THE AGE OF CHARLES I

The Age of Charles I

PAINTING IN ENGLAND
1620-1649

Oliver Millar

THE TATE GALLERY

1972

Published by order of the Trustees 1972
for the Exhibition of 15 November 1972 – 14 January 1973

Exclusively distributed in France and Italy by Idea Books
24 rue du 4 Septembre, Paris (2e), and Via Maddalena 1, 20122 Milan

Jacket/Cover illustrations: *front*: Henrietta Maria (cat.196)
back: Charles I at his Trial (cat.175)
Frontis: Landscape with St George and the Dragon (cat.84 *detail*)

Copyright ©1972 The Tate Gallery
ISBN 0 900874 55 4 Cloth
ISBN 0 900874 54 6 Paper
Designed and published by the
Tate Gallery Publications Department
Millbank, London SW1P 4RG
and printed in Great Britain by
Balding & Mansell Ltd, London and Wisbech

Foreword

This is the second in a series of exhibitions devoted to a particular period of earlier British painting of which the first, *The Elizabethan Image*, was held in the winter of 1969–70.

For the present exhibition Mr Oliver Millar, Surveyor of the Queen's Pictures, has been responsible both for the selection of the works and for writing the catalogue. His introduction fully explains the scope of the exhibition to which he has devoted a great deal of his valuable time.

As always, it is to the many lenders, whether private collectors or public institutions in this country and abroad, that we are most indebted. Indeed, without their generous co-operation such an exhibition would be impossible. Their names are given at the end of this catalogue. Of those who have lent extensively from their collections I would mention particularly Her Majesty The Queen from whom we have borrowed a large number of paintings, miniatures, drawings and etchings, the Trustees of the Chatsworth Settlement (Devonshire Collection) and the Trustees of the British Museum.

I would also like to thank the designers of the exhibition, Stefan Buzas and Alan Irvine, for their excellent solution to the usual problem of displaying a large number of works in a very limited space.

We are also grateful to those who have kindly lent ektachromes for use in the catalogue, in particular works belonging to Her Majesty The Queen and the National Portrait Gallery, London.

NORMAN REID

Introduction

The ideal Charles I exhibition can only be mounted in the imagination. It would involve asking for the loan of some of the most famous pictures in the world; and even if it was possible to hang together once more the pictures which the King placed in the Bear Gallery, the Privy Lodging Rooms or the Cabinet Room at Whitehall, or in the grandest rooms at Hampton Court, Greenwich, and Somerset House, we do not know in detail what the rooms themselves looked like. We could not see the pictures against the furnishings, hangings, curtains and carpets which originally set them off. In this exhibition, therefore, no attempt has been made to reassemble Charles I's great collection of renaissance pictures and works of art. Only a small display of photographs outside the exhibition will perhaps serve to remind visitors of the quality of the collections which the King was assembling before the outbreak of the Civil War.

The sophisticated tastes of the King and the other Caroline collectors, their avid enthusiasm for classical and renaissance works of art, their interest in contemporary art on the Continent—the links established with studios in Spain, the Netherlands, Italy and France—and their patronage of some of the most celebrated contemporary foreign artists and craftsmen, inevitably affected the development of the arts in England. It is, of course, impossible in the space available to give a complete picture of artistic activity in this country in this period. Inevitably, for example, a small amount of sculpture is all that can be assembled, but a visit to Westminster Abbey will give the student a complete survey of contemporary developments in monumental and figure sculpture. The achievement of Inigo Jones, perhaps the most significant figure in the flowering of connoisseurship at the Jacobean and Caroline court, has deliberately only been sketched in the present exhibition because it is to be demonstrated in detail in the commemorative exhibition to be held in the Banqueting House in 1973. The tapestries woven at the royal factory at Mortlake, which are so important a manifestation of early Stuart royal patronage and stimulated the art of design in this country on a large scale, can conveniently be studied in the newly opened Tapestry Court at the Victoria and Albert Museum. In these fields, as in the field of painting with which this exhibition is primarily concerned, one sees the influence, on artists working in England, of the works of art acquired by the 'Whitehall group' and of the artists they attracted to England.

The purpose of this exhibition is to show, as a sequel to *The Elizabethan Image* held at the Tate Gallery in the winter of 1969–70, the principal tendencies in English painting between the middle years of the reign of James I and the execution of his son in 1649. The crux of the theme is the time spent in London by Anthony van Dyck: perhaps the most important and fruitful episode—a veritable watershed—in the history of English painting. The pictures in the early part of the exhibition demonstrate the advances made in portrait-painting from the rigidly patterned designs, which visitors will remember from *The Elizabethan Image*, towards the accomplished, full-blooded and modern style of the painters encouraged by such patrons as Prince Charles and the Earl of Arundel to try their fortune in London. Most important: contacts were being developed between the English court and the studio of Rubens in Antwerp, where the young Van Dyck in particular was attracting attention. Rubens's contacts with the Prince, Arundel and the Duke of Buckingham are demonstrated in a number of paintings and drawings; and a later group of paintings, drawings and sketches illustrate his visit to the court of Charles I and something of his preliminary work on the ceiling which he was commissioned to paint for the Banqueting House, where it miraculously survives as the most significant monument to Charles I's patronage as well as a great painter's tribute to the tastes and ideals of a particularly perceptive patron.

The nature of Van Dyck's work at the English court; the transformation which he wrought in the practice of the portrait-painter in England; the qualities of perception and allusion, the flowing patterns, fine technique and lovely colour, which all seem in a different world even from the accomplished Daniel Mytens; these are aspects of the period which the exhibition aims to demonstrate. It is equally important to notice, on the one hand, the survival through the period of a more provincial idiom as well as, on the other, the almost immediate influence that Van Dyck's style and repertory exerted in England. A group of pictures by William Dobson, the most important native-born painter working 'in large' in England in the seventeenth century, shows how a painter could benefit from the influence of Van Dyck and of pictures in the great Caroline collections; but shows also that the Civil War and Interregnum, by destroying the fabric of Caroline court culture, destroyed also so much of the potential influence, on the arts in England, of the activities of Charles I and his fellow-collectors. The early work of Peter Lely, however, is a corrective (if one was needed) to the view that painting in the last years of the Civil War and during the Commonwealth is universally sombre; and reveals also something of the significance of the patronage of men like the Earl of Northumberland who had been patrons at Whitehall in the 1630s but remained in London during the conflict. Pictures by other foreigners, such as Honthorst, Orazio Gentileschi and his daughter Artemesia, who had worked at the English court, indicate the King's and his consort's liking for aspects of early baroque painting in the decorative field; and the popularity of little subject-pictures by such painters as Hendrick van Steenwyck illustrates, by contrast, that delight in the meticulous and the highly wrought which is so marked a feature of taste in England under the Stuarts.

Portrait-painting dominates the *Age of Charles I* as it did *The Elizabethan Image*, but there are to be seen also the germs of landscape and topographical painting and drawing in England: in, for example, the drawings and prints by Hollar, landscape drawings and views of London by De Jongh or, in a more personal vein, the studies of landscape and plants by Van Dyck. A group of portrait medals has been included, principally because of their iconographical value. There is, finally, a large selection of portrait miniatures. They are among the most beautiful creations of the period, confronting us with amazing intensity with the men and women of the time; and they illustrate in microcosm some of the changes that come over the English portrait in the early Stuart period.

The catalogue has been so arranged as to define briefly certain themes and artistic personalities in the exhibition. In the catalogue standard art-historical material has been kept to a minimum, though references are given to where such material may be found. It has seemed more important to suggest, within its context, the significance of the individual works of art.

I should like to thank Sir Norman Reid most warmly for inviting me to select the works for the exhibition. I hope that it will have added to the knowledge of early British painting, to which exhibitions at the Tate Gallery are making such valuable contributions. I am very grateful to Miss Ruth Rattenbury for the efficiency with which she has borne such a large part of the administrative burden involved in an exhibition of this size; to Mr Alan Irvine for the lucidity and good taste of his lay-out; to Mr Iain Bain for the care he has lavished on the catalogue; and to Mrs Gilbert Cousland for typing a very large part of the catalogue.

O. M.

Abbreviations

Burchard and d'Hulst L. Burchard and R.-A. d'Hulst, *Rubens Drawings* (Brussels, 1963)

Burl. Mag. *The Burlington Magazine*

Croft-Murray E. Croft-Murray and P. Hulton, *Catalogue of British Drawings*, vol. I (1960)

Glück G. Glück, *Van Dyck*, Klassiker der Kunst (Stuttgart, 1931)

Goulding R. W. Goulding, 'The Welbeck Abbey Miniatures', *Walpole Society*, vol. IV (1916)

Hervey M. F. S. Hervey, *The Life, Correspondence . . . of Thomas Howard, Earl of Arundel* (1921)

Held J. S. Held, *Rubens Selected Drawings* (1959)

Hind A. M. Hind, *Catalogue of Drawings by Dutch and Flemish Artists . . . in the British Museum*, vol. II (1923)

Ter Kuile O. Ter Kuile, 'Daniel Mijtens', *Nederlands Kunsthistorisch Jaarboek*, vol. XX (1969), pp. 1–106

Magurn *The Letters of Peter Paul Rubens*, ed. R. S. Magurn (Cambridge, Mass., 1955)

M.-H. M. Mauquoy-Hendrickx, *L'Iconographie d'Antoine van Dyck* (Brussels, 1956)

M.I. *Medallic Illustrations*

Millar, *Tudor, Stuart* O. Millar, *The Tudor, Stuart and Early Georgian Pictures in the Collection of H.M. The Queen* (1963)

Oldenbourg E. Oldenbourg, *P. P. Rubens*, Klassiker der Kunst (Stuttgart etc., 1921)

Oppé A. P. Oppé, *English Drawings . . . at Windsor Castle* (1950)

Parthey G. Parthey, *Wenzel Hollar* (Berlin, 1853)

Sainsbury W. N. Sainsbury, *Original Unpublished Papers . . .* (1859)

Van der Doort 'Abraham van der Doort's Catalogue of the Collections of Charles I', ed. O. Millar, *Walpole Society*, vol. XXXVII (1960)

Vey H. Vey, *Die Zeichnungen Anton van Dycks* (Brussels, 1962)

Whinney M. Whinney, *Sculpture in Britain 1530 to 1830* (1964)

Whinney and Millar M. Whinney and O. Millar, *English Art 1625–1714* (1957)

The Duke of York

Charles I was born at Dunfermline Palace on 19 November 1600, the second son and youngest child of King James VI and Queen Anne of Denmark. On 24 March 1603, at the death of Elizabeth I, King James succeeded to the throne of England. The Union of the Crowns, which his son was to cause Rubens to depict on the ceiling of his Banqueting House, was the greatest moment in King James's life:

> Shake hands with Union, O thou mighty state,
> Now thou art all Great-Britaine . . .
> No wall of Adrian serves to seperate
> Our mutuall love, nor our obedience,
> Being subjects all to one Imperial Prince.

Prince Charles followed his parents southwards in 1604. On 6 January 1605 he was created Duke of York. As a delicate and tongue-tied child he grew up in the shadow of his charming sister Elizabeth and his dashing brother Henry, Prince of Wales. It was probably under his influence of his mother, Anne of Denmark, and his brother that the little Duke of York began to develop his feeling for works of art: a feeling which was to make him the most discerning patron and collector who has ever graced the British throne. His mother built up a good collection of pictures, principally at Somerset House and Oatlands, and was also a lavish patroness of Inigo Jones. From soon after her husband's accession Jones was engaged on the production of the series of court masques, from the *Masque of Blackness* which Ben Jonson wrote for performance at Whitehall on Twelfth Night, 1605; after his return from a second visit to Italy and his appointment as Surveyor of the King's Works in September 1615, Jones designed for the Queen an ornamental gateway in the orchard wall at Oatlands and the Queen's House at Greenwich which was begun in 1616 and which was to be enriched by her younger son with commissions from some of the finest decorative artists in Europe.

Inigo Jones had produced earlier the sets and costumes for *Prince Henry's Barriers* by Ben Jonson, which was produced in the old Banqueting House on Twelfth Night, 1610. It was the martial Prince's first public appearance in arms, at which he and six companions challenged fifty-eight defendants in combat. The Prince's enthusiasm for arms, armour and martial pursuits is glitteringly demonstrated in Isaac Oliver's miniature (179). But he also showed that he regarded an interest in artists and craftsmen, in books and works of art, as an important part of the complete gentleman's personality. Inigo Jones, who had been appointed in 1610 Surveyor of Works to the Prince, fitted up for him a gallery, and probably a library also, at St. James's in which the Prince's collections could be placed. Pictures and other works of art were given to him by such friends as the Earl of Arundel (1) and were presented to him by neighbouring governments. He owned portraits of contemporary rulers such as the King of France and the Princes of Orange. Good Dutch sea-pieces were given to him in 1610 by an embassy from the States-General. Portraits and other presents would be exchanged during negotiations for a marriage between the Prince and a Savoy, Medici, Bourbon or

Spanish princess. A taste for Venetian painting would perhaps have been encouraged by his father's favourite, the Earl of Somerset. In 1611 the Prince was attempting to induce Michiel van Miereveld of Delft, regarded at that time as 'the most excellent Painter of all the Low-Countries' to enter his service, although his Household already contained, in addition to Jones, a painter, a limner of pictures, a jeweller and a mender of tapestries and, as Keeper of his Cabinet Room, the Dutchman Abraham van der Doort. He also had in his service two foreign architects, Salamon de Caux and the Florentine Constantino dei Servi. The Venetian ambassador reported in January 1611 that the Prince's interests extended to ordering many gardens and fountains. Negotiations with foreign painters, and the pursuit of pictures overseas, would have been carried out for the Prince by envoys, such as Sir Henry Wotton and Sir Dudley Carleton, or by such sensitive soldiers serving in the Low Countries as Sir Edward Conway and Sir Edward Cecil, who would be found among the patrons of Miereveld. The Prince's tastes no doubt owed much to the influence of the Earl of Arundel and Inigo Jones.

On the death of Anne of Denmark in 1617 her pictures passed to her younger son; and at the untimely death of Prince Henry, five years earlier, his collections, and his cabinet at St. James's, had also been inherited by Prince Charles. Not long before Prince Henry's death, when he received a present of small bronzes from the Grand Duke of Tuscany, Sir Edward Cecil had remarked that 'il piccolo cavallino' would do well for the younger Prince: perhaps a recognition that the little boy was becoming as interested in the arts as he was in horsemanship (information from Miss Katrina Watson).

The Earl of Arundel

Thomas Howard, Earl of Arundel, was a grandson of the 4th Duke of Norfolk and son of Philip, Earl of Arundel, who had died in the Tower in 1595. His austerity and grandeur may have developed partly as a reaction against the grim times through which his family were living as a result of the execution of his grandfather in 1572. The Earl was, however, restored in blood in 1604 and in 1621 was made Earl Marshal. He was in favour with Prince Henry and involved with the growth of his collections; he performed in masques and was closely associated with Inigo Jones. In 1607 Arundel House was restored to him and he ultimately inherited pictures and works of art from his Fitzalan forbears and his Lumley relations. His marriage in 1605 to Aletheia Talbot, daughter of the Earl of Shrewsbury and grand-daughter of 'Bess of Hardwick', brought him increased resources as well as a kindred enthusiasm for collecting and foreign travel. He became the most significant, and possibly the most serious and influential, of the patrons and connoisseurs whose tastes developed during the reign of James I.

He travelled in the Low Countries and also formed a deep affection for Italy, 'the humour and manners of which nation he seemed most to like and approve, and affected to imitate'. In 1613, after escorting the newly-married Princess Elizabeth and the King of Bohemia to Heidelberg, he went to Italy, where he remained until 1614, excavating and studying works of art and remains, often in company with Inigo Jones. In addition to the marbles he acquired in Italy and the Levant, celebrated in the history of English taste as the Arundel Marbles, the Earl assembled at Arundel House a superb collection of pictures in which he showed a special liking for northern painting and a feeling for drawings. The famous collection of Leonardo drawings at Windsor was brought to England by Arundel; he was also particularly fond of the drawings of Parmigianino. He had admitted to a 'foolish curiosity' for the work of Holbein, who had painted a number of his ancestors at the Tudor court. His agents were working on his behalf all over Europe, and his ruthlessly acquisitive methods provoked angry reactions from rival collectors, of whom he was often jealous. In 1618 the Countess of Bedford described 'a tricke my Lo. of Arundell putt upon me yesterday to the cusning me of some pictures promised me'.

He was a discerning patron of contemporary artists and craftsmen: 'one that Loved and favored all artes and artists in a greate measure, and was the bringer of them in to Englande'. In 1620, for example, Rubens described him as *uno delli quatro evangelisti e soportator del nostro arte;* he was clearly interested in getting Van Dyck over to London in that year; he sat to him during his first visit to England and was instrumental in procuring for him a pass to travel to Italy early in the following year; Mytens owed a great deal to Arundel's patronage on his arrival here (see No.3); the Earl patronised Dieussart and Fanelli; and in 1636, on a mission to the Emperor of Austria, Arundel enlisted Hollar into his service.

1

2

4   3

DANIEL MYTENS (c.1590–1647)

1. **Thomas Howard, Earl of Arundel (1585–1646)**
   Oil on canvas: $81\frac{1}{2} \times 50$ in.
   The Duke of Norfolk

2. **Aletheia Talbot, Countess of Arundel (d.1654)**
   Oil on canvas: $81\frac{1}{2} \times 50$ in.
   The Duke of Norfolk

   In his letter of 18 August 1618 (see No.3) Mytens referred to 'those great pictures' of the Earl and Countess which he could not persuade the Earl to part with 'by reason they doe leyke his honr so well that he will keep them'. The portraits had probably been recently finished and are Mytens's earliest documented full-lengths. They show already the solidity of form and freedom of touch characteristic of Mytens's style in contrast to the style in which his predecessors at the court had been working; but he is not yet able to place his sitters convincingly in space.

   The setting of both portraits is Arundel House. The Earl points with his Earl Marshal's baton to the Sculpture Gallery on the first floor, in which he had recently placed some of the statues which he had brought back in 1614 from the second visit to Italy. Much of his statuary was also displayed in the beautiful gardens at Arundel House. Behind the Countess in No.2 is a gallery on the ground floor of Arundel House, lined with family portraits, almost all in the austere black frames which were popular at that period. Both portraits are valuable for their illustration of the methods of display of works of art. The portrait of the Earl foreshadows Nanteuil's well-known plate of Cardinal Mazarin seated in front of his *Galerie Haute* of pictures and sculpture (Hervey, p.143; Ter Kuile, pp.43–46 (1, 2)).

3. **Thomas Howard, Earl of Arundel, and Aletheia Talbot, Countess of Arundel**
   Oil on canvas: 34×48 in. Formerly in the collection of Oliver Watney at Cornbury Park, sold at Christie's, 7 July 1967 (64).
   The Duke of Norfolk

   The canvas may well be 'that picture or portrait of the Ld of Arundel and his lady, to gether in a small forme ... rowled up in a smal case', which Mytens sent to Sir Dudley Carleton on 18 August 1618. He had tried unsuccessfully to persuade the Earl to part with the big full-lengths (Nos.1, 2); the Earl asked him 'to make these in a smaller forme, who I trust your Honr will accept and exteem as a smal presents

donne for my Ly of Arundel and for mij paines and ceare I have done therein to the most of mij pouwer.' Thanking Arundel for his present, Carleton wrote on 28 September: 'Those I have lately receaved from yor Ldps painter in one table, I humbly thanke yor Ldp. for, and I wish he had been so happie in hitting my Lady as he hath perfectly done your Ldp, but I observe it generally in woemens pictures, they have as much disadvantage in ye art as they have advantage in nature' (Hervey, p.143; Ter Kuile, pp.25, 46–47 (3)).

4. **Henry Wriothesley, 3rd Earl of Southampton (1573–1624)**
   Oil on panel: 31×24 in. Dated: *anno.161* [?8] and signed *DMytens* (initials in monogram). Probably passed by inheritance from the sitter's daughter Penelope, who married the 2nd Lord Spencer in 1617.
   The Earl Spencer

   The patron of Shakespeare and associate of the 2nd Earl of Essex. No.4 is the earliest recorded signed and dated work by Mytens; with it can be grouped fairly confidently a portrait at Tyninghame of the 1st Earl of Haddington painted in the same year. The portrait is more accomplished and modern than the work of the more traditional painters at court and in design and character is indistinguishable from the conventional Dutch portrait-style in which Mytens had been brought up. It can be compared, in this military context, to Miereveld's portrait of Sir Horace Vere (No.5) (Ter Kuile, pp.95–96 (100)).

Attributed to MICHIEL VAN MIEREVELD (1567–1641)

5. **Horace, Lord Vere of Tilbury (1565–1635)**
   Oil on panel: $34\frac{1}{4} \times 25\frac{1}{4}$ in. Inscribed, below the arms of the Vere family, *ÆTATIS. 61./ 1629*
   The National Portrait Gallery, London

   One of the most famous English soldiers of the day, under whose command many of the future officers in the Civil War (on both sides of the quarrel) received their training. He was one of the most trusted commanders fighting under the Princes of Orange in the wars in the Low Countries and in 1620 was placed by James I in command of an expeditionary force sent to assist the Elector Palatine. The little landscape below the portrait shows, presumably, his tent with an arquebusier on guard, between

5

piles of military equipment, and a battle or skirmish in the background.

The design is very close to Miereveld's portrait of Vere, of which one version, formerly in the Craven collection, is signed and dated 1623; but the two types are not in fact identical and No.5, which is richer in handling, should perhaps be attributed to Jan Anthonisz. van Ravesteyn. It could have been painted in The Hague before Vere's departure to the siege of Bois-le-Duc in April 1629 or after the fall of the town in September. In the present context No.5 is placed to show how close portraits painted in England, by Mytens (e.g., No.4) and Cornelius Johnson, are in design and mood to contemporary and slightly earlier portraits by fashionable portrait-painters in Holland. Portraits of English commanders are to be found beside those of the other officers in the service of the Prince of Orange or the Queen of Bohemia (i.e., in the set formerly in the Craven collection but now partly dispersed); a prototype of such a series would be the set of portraits by Ravesteyn of officers in the Prince of Orange's service (now in the Mauritshuis and dated 1611–16); and Sir Horace's widow kept the set of full-lengths (by various hands and now dispersed) of her husband's fellow-officers to 'at once guard and adorn Kirby-hall in Essex' (D. Piper, *Catalogue of Seventeenth-Century Portraits*, National Portrait Gallery (1963), pp.361–2 (818)).

MICHIEL VAN MIEREVELD (1567–1641)

6. **Sir Dudley Carleton, Viscount Dorchester (1573–1632)**
    Oil on panel: $25\frac{1}{4} \times 21$ in. Signed: *M. Mierevelt* and inscribed: *Ætatis 54/A°.1628.*
    John Carleton, Esq.

    Carleton was active in buying works of art for English collections. He realised that advancement in his career would be hastened by his and his wife's 'service to our chiefe persons at home who looke after' works of art of all kinds, particularly the Duke of Buckingham: 'since I am', as he wrote in 1617, 'by mischance made a master of such curiosities'. He was the most significant figure in the development, through diplomatic channels, of links between the English court and the studios of painters in the Low Countries. As early as 1611, while he was in Venice, he had been looking for pictures for Prince Henry and Lord Salisbury. He was Ambassador to The Hague from 1616 to 1625 and from the earliest days of this appointment was in touch with painters. In the autumn of 1616 he made a 'pettie progresse' to Haarlem, Leiden, Amsterdam and Utrecht. At Haarlem he met Cornelis Cornelisz. Vroom and Goltzius. In 1621 he reported on Honthorst's growing reputation. His knowledge of the studios in Antwerp, and his negotiations with Rubens (see No.15) in 1616 and in 1618 were no less significant. He was closely associated with the Earl of Arundel (see No.3). To Charles I Carleton gave pictures by Torrentius and *Daniel in the Lions' Den*, one of the pictures he had secured during his negotiations with Rubens.

SIR PETER PAUL RUBENS
(1577–1640)

7. **Robin, the Earl of Arundel's Dwarf**
Black, red and white chalk and pen and ink, on
paper: $16\frac{1}{16} \times 10\frac{1}{8}$ in. There are colour-notes in
Rubens's hand: the mantle may be red satin
and the breeches red velvet: brown velvet
(twice): red: yellow: red: black: red lining.
The Nationalmuseum, Stockholm

The Countess of Arundel set out on a foreign
tour in June 1620. In July she was in Antwerp,
where she sat to Rubens for the great portrait, now
in Munich (Oldenbourg, p.200), in which she is
accompanied by her jester, Robin and a gentleman
who is probably Sir Dudley Carleton. The large
group makes a fascinating contrast with No.2. It is
the first portrait by Rubens of an English sitter and
is an early masterpiece of baroque state portraiture.
In a letter to the Earl, written from Antwerp on
17 July 1620, probably by the Countess's secretary
Francesco Vercellini, Rubens's progress on the
group is described. By that date Rubens had finished,
from a sitting, the likeness of the Countess and those
of the dwarf, the jester and the dog. He had drawn
on paper the postures and costumes and had ordered
a canvas on which he would copy with his own hand
what he had done. It is not, however, impossible
that Van Dyck worked with Rubens on the big
canvas; the possibility of Van Dyck's coming to
London is broached in the same letter (Held, pp.
31–32, 44, 136; Burchard and d'Hulst, No.127).

SIR ANTHONY VAN DYCK
(1599–1641)

8. **George Gage (c.1592–1638)** (*identity uncertain*) **with two Servants (?) supporting an Antique Statue of a Woman**
Oil on canvas: $45\frac{1}{4} \times 44\frac{11}{16}$ in.
The Trustees of the National Gallery, London

The identity of the sitter has for long been in
doubt and the authorship of the picture has recently
been cast in doubt. It seems, however, to be consistent with Van Dyck's style, *c*.1620–1, on the eve of
his departure for Italy but after he had moved away
from the more conventional, enclosed and static
repertory of designs which he had evolved for his
earliest portraits of *c*.1616–18. It is feasible to compare it, for example, with the group-portraits, in
which there is a new freedom of paint and relaxation

of pose, in Detroit and Budapest (Glück, pp.96, 113). The arms carved on the ledge on which the sitter leans are those of the Gage family, whose crest is the ram's head. There is a strong possibility that the portrait represents George Gage, a diplomat and 'a graceful person, of good address, well skill'd in musick, painting and architecture': a good example of the type of civilised, cosmopolitan Englishman, of vaguely diplomatic status, who played so important a part at this period in establishing links between London and artistic centres on the Continent. In 1616 Gage was, on Carleton's behalf, negotiating with Rubens for pictures and was involved in the exchange between the two men of pictures and antiquities. He knew the Antwerp studios and secured for Carleton pictures by Bruegel, Vranckx and Snyders: 'makinge your severall painters to out-strippe themselves in what they have done for y^w'. Early in 1620, when he was planning to visit Rubens again in Antwerp, he could have met the young Van Dyck and may even have played some part in per-suading him to visit London (O. Millar in *Burl. Mag.*, vol. CXI (1969), pp.414–17; G. Martin, *The Flemish School*, National Gallery (1970), pp.58–61 (49)).

The Duke of Buckingham

George Villiers, son of Sir George Villiers of Brokesby, rose rapidly to favour at the court of James I. In 1614 he was appointed Cupbearer; by 1618 he was Marquess and in 1623 he was raised to the Dukedom. He held many of the great offices of state.

The Duke built up at York House, which was granted to him in March 1624 and which he altered at vast cost, a spectacular collection of pictures in a very short space of time and principally with the help and advice of Balthasar Gerbier. Writing in February 1625, Gerbier told his patron that 'out of all the amateurs, and Princes and Kings, there is not one who has collected in forty years as many pictures as your Excellency has collected in five.' In contrast with the austere and more learned tastes of Arundel, Buckingham said himself that he was 'not so fond of antiquity to court it in a deformed or misshapen stone'; but he had a special love for Venetian painting of the sixteenth century, in which he followed the tastes of the Earl of Somerset, his predecessor in James I's affections, and helped to form the tastes of the young Prince Charles. In 1621, for example, Gerbier sent over to Buckingham from Venice a consignment which included Titian's great *Ecce Homo* (now in Vienna); and the Duke's collection of Venetian pictures would have influenced the young Van Dyck on his visit to London in 1620–21, when it seems that Buckingham gave him at least one commission (see No.10). In Spain in 1623 Buckingham's acquisitions included Giovanni da Bologna's *Samson and the Philistine*, now in the Victoria and Albert Museum.

Among living painters, whom he met on journeys to the Continent or patronised at home, the Duke had a special liking for such painters as Manfredi and Honthorst, to whom he sat in 1628, Orazio Gentileschi (see No.119) and, above all, Rubens, whom the Duke also met in Paris and whom he persuaded to sell a large collection of pictures and statues. When Rubens was in England, he wrote to Peiresc on 9 August 1629: 'when it comes to fine pictures by the hands of first-class masters, I have never seen such a large number in one place as in the royal palace and in the gallery of the late Duke of Buckingham' (Magurn, p. 322).

9

MICHIEL VAN MIEREVELD (1567–1641)

9. **George Villiers, 1st Duke of Buckingham (1592–1628)**
Oil on panel: 30 × 25 in. Signed and dated: *M. Mierevelt ad sui ipsius/[?principale] depinxit. Sir Gyles Isham, Bt.*
Of all the portraits of the Duke ('a man to draw an angel by') Miereveld's perhaps gives the most vivid impression of his opulent appearance. Buckingham's accounts include, in the period of his embassy to the Low Countries, from September 1625 to July 1626, payment of £60 'To the Picture drawer', who may have been Miereveld. It was a popular design; of a number of versions at least one is signed and dated 1625; in the following year W. J. Delff published his fine engraving of the type.

SIR ANTHONY VAN DYCK (1599–1641)

10. **The Continence of Scipio**
Oil on canvas: 72 × 91½ in., repr. on p.17
The Governing Body of Christ Church, Oxford
No.10 is probably to be associated with a picture in the Duchess of Buckingham's collection: 'one Great Piece being Scipio' by Van Dyck, hanging in the hall at York House in 1635; a payment to 'Vandyke the picture drawer' had been made by Endymion Porter on Buckingham's behalf, but the date of the payment and the sum involved are unspecified. Stylistically, however, No.10 could well have been painted for Buckingham in the months spent by Van Dyck in London between November 1620 and February 1621. If so, it would provide an early example of a Jacobean connoisseur commissioning a picture far more sophisticated than usual and at a court where the demand was still almost exclusively for portraits. The design is closely based on Rubens (the material is conveniently presented by Agnes Czobor in *Burl. Mag.*, vol. CIX (1967), pp. 351–5), but the two-dimensional rhythms in the design, the hurriedly drawn and insubstantial forms and the confused spatial relationships in the groups are all typical of Van Dyck at this period when he was moving away from Rubens's orbit. The colour and the frieze-like composition on a narrow stage may reflect the influence of Venetian painting on Van Dyck who would have seen at York House, for example, the Duke's superb series of Veroneses of which seven are now in Vienna (O. Millar in *Burl. Mag.*, vol. XCIII (1951), pp. 125–6; J. Byam Shaw, *Paintings by Old Masters at Christ Church, Oxford* (1967), No. 245).

Sir Peter Paul Rubens
(1577–1640)

11. **George Villiers, 1st Duke of Buckingham (1592–1628)**

Black, red and white chalk; ink on the eyes; on paper: $15\frac{1}{16} \times 10\frac{1}{2}$ in. Inscribed later with the names of the artist and the sitter.

The Albertina, Vienna

Drawn in Paris in 1625, where Rubens was working on the Medici cycle when the Duke attended the marriage by proxy of Charles I and Princess Henrietta Maria. The Duke whose 'caprice and arrogance' Rubens thought dangerous, arrived in Paris on 14 May. The drawing was used by Rubens in painting the great equestrian portrait (now destroyed) of the Duke (Oldenbourg, p.267) which hung in the Great Chamber at York House: 'Reuben. My Lord Duke on Horseback'. The Duke's expenses in France in 1625 included £500 'Given to Mr Rubens for drawing his L^{ps} picture on horsback' (B.M., Add. MSS. 12528, f.23) (Held, pp.77, 138).

11

12. **The Duke of Buckingham escorted by Minerva and Mercury to the Temple of *Virtus* (?)**

Oil on panel: $25\frac{3}{16} \times 25\frac{1}{8}$; the painted area is roughly circular; the spandrels are filled in with black paint.

The Trustees of the National Gallery, London

A sketch for the 'great piece for the ceiling of my Lord's Closett' at York House by Rubens. The 'great piece' was later at Osterley, but was destroyed by fire in 1949. The design was formerly described as an Apotheosis of the Duke, but an earlier sketch for the ceiling shows him climbing up to the temple, assisted by Minerva and heralded by Fame. There are signs of *pentimenti* in No.12, but it establishes fairly closely the design and iconography of the final ceiling: with *Virtus* and Abundance awaiting the Duke, the three Graces offering him a crown of flowers and Envy attempting to pull him down. The anonymous writer of *Felton Commended* said that 'Antwerpian Rubens' best skill made him soare, Ravish't by heavenly powers, unto the skie, Opening and ready him to deifie In a bright blisfull pallace, fayrie ile'. Envy had figured in pursuit of the Duke in a masque presented at York House to the King and Queen before the Duke's departure for the Isle of Rhé; and in the epitaph in the chapel in which he was buried the Duke's widow described him as the 'spotless Sacrifice to ravenous Envy'.

12

The Duke had met Rubens in Paris in 1625. At that time, having seen the Medici cycle, he may have commissioned the ceiling for York House at the same time as he sat for his portrait on horseback (see No.11) (G. Martin in *Burl. Mag.*, vol. CVIII (1966), pp.613–18; *The Flemish School*, National Gallery (1970), pp.147–53 (187)). Although the quality of the sketch is close to the period of the Medici cycle, and to a sketch in the Liechtenstein collection in which the principal figure is probably Marie de Medici, the iconography, for an English sitter, has obvious links with the *Apotheosis of James I* (No.39) for the ceiling of the Banqueting House.

ABRAHAM VAN BLYENBERCH (*fl.*1617–22)

13. **Benjamin Jonson (1573(?)–1637)**
     Oil on canvas: $18\frac{1}{2} \times 16\frac{1}{2}$ in.
     The National Portrait Gallery, London
     Poet and dramatist, associated with Inigo Jones in the production of masques at court between their *Masque of Blackness* for Anne of Denmark in 1605 and the final bitter quarrel between the two men in 1631, after the production of *Chloridia*, danced by Henrietta Maria and her ladies.
     Blyenberch, who was in Antwerp in 1622, had been recorded in London between 1617 and 1621. He had worked on designs for tapestries and painted the Prince of Wales, Lord Ancram (No.14) and the 3rd Earl of Pembroke. On the basis of this small *œuvre* his style seems rather variable, but the portrait of Jonson could well be identified with: 'Blyenberke. A Picture of Ben Johnson', which appears in the inventory of the Buckingham collection of 1635 and would probably have been painted for the Duke, *c.*1618. It became, as a type, the standard portrait of the poet, used as the source of a number of derivative pieces and of the engraving by Robert Vaughan, printed not later than 1627 (R. Strong, *Tudor and Jacobean Portraits*, National Portrait Gallery (1969), vol. I, pp.183–4 (2752)).

14. **Robert Kerr, 1st Earl of Ancram (1578–1654)**
     Oil on canvas: 42×39 in. Signed and dated: *AV. blijenberch/ . . . / 1618·*; inscribed: *Sin ocasion nadie se senato* and twice with the sitter's name and the date 1618.
     The Marquess of Lothian
     Sir Robert was Captain of the Bodyguard to James I and a Gentleman of the Bedchamber to Charles I. He was one of the most enlightened men at the court of James I: a close friend of John Donne, who gave him his portrait. He was particularly interested in Dutch painting and died in exile and poverty in Amsterdam. He was sent by Charles I to The Hague on a mission of condolence to Elizabeth, Queen of Bohemia, after her eldest son had been drowned in 1629. In Holland Kerr met Constantine Huygens, the Prince of Orange's secretary; and, presumably through Huygens, received as a present for Charles I three pictures: one probably by Lievens and the other two by Rembrandt, a *Self-portrait* (probably the one now in the Walker Art Gallery, Liverpool), and the portrait of the old woman which is still in the royal collection. It was through Kerr's embassy, therefore, and friendship with Huygens that connoisseurs at Whitehall had an early glimpse of the genius of the young men at Leiden.

Stylistically Blyenberch's portrait of Ancram is, within the Anglo-Netherlandish context, less fully modelled, but perhaps more refined, than Mytens and more sensitive in feeling and touch than Van Somer.

13

14

The Prince of Wales

Prince Charles had been devoted to his brother and revered his memory. When he came to assemble a set of family portraits in the Cross Gallery at Somerset House he caused Van Dyck to paint a posthumous full-length, based on Isaac Oliver's miniature (No.179) of the Prince 'of famous memory'. Observers thought he had more understanding than his brother: 'in behaviour sober, grave and sweet'. To the influence of Arundel, Jones and Prince Henry on the formation of his tastes, must be added the increasing influence of his father's favourite, George Villiers, who, like Robert Kerr before him, had a special liking for Venetian painting of the sixteenth century. As early as 1609 the Venetian ambassador in London reported to the Doge and Senate that Prince Charles was hoping to visit Venice; and to a character study of the Prince, written in September 1622, the ambassador, after a description of his appearance, his skill at horsemanship, dancing and the use of arms, added: 'he loves old paintings, especially those of our province and city'.

Although the journey to Spain with Buckingham in 1623—the Spanish Marriage Venture—was a political fiasco, the experience was of importance for its influence on the Prince and his companions: Buckingham, Gerbier, Endymion Porter, Lord Denbigh and William Murray, who were members of the 'Whitehall group' of collectors, connoisseurs and expert advisers. In Spain the Prince bought pictures, was painted by Velázquez and, in the collections inherited by his prospective brother-in-law, the young Philip IV, saw for the first time a superb collection of renaissance works of art: an experience which left an abiding impression on his mind and strengthened his special love for the work of Titian. On the eve of his departure for England Philip IV formally presented to him the *Venus of the Pardo*. While he was in Madrid the Prince of Wales gave orders for the purchase of Raphael's *Cartoons*; and he had for some time been in touch with Rubens. Before his accession to the throne on 27 March 1625 he had already built up a most impressive collection of pictures: contemporary portraits by Bunel, Mytens and Van Somer, with masterpieces by Van der Goes, Rubens, Holbein, Titian and Tintoretto.

The Prince was becoming a discerning patron of contemporary painters. He had sat to Hilliard and employed Isaac Oliver and his son Peter. As a boy he had been painted officially by Gheeraedts and by Robert Peake, the Serjeant Painter who had been in his brother's service; but he obviously realised that the portrait-painters recently arrived from the Netherlands, Van Somer, Blyenberch and Mytens, were more accomplished. He seems, in particular, to have taken Mytens under his protection. In the winter of 1620–21 he would have met at court the young Van Dyck.

The Prince stands, therefore, at the heart of that group of collectors and patrons whose activities up to the outbreak of the Civil War constitute the most spectacular moment in the history of English taste. The reign of the peace-loving James I saw a flowering of artistic consciousness which had not been possible in the reign of the parsimonious Elizabeth I, when cultural links with the Continent were inevitably affected by the course of war, internal strife and religious persecution. Under the early Stuarts contacts were developed with studios and workshops all over the Continent, from

Spain to the Low Countries, from Copenhagen to Rome. Painters, sculptors and craftsmen were encouraged, regardless of religious prejudice, to come to London; and the same contacts, the same local knowledge, and the experience of the artists themselves, were used by the collectors who were building up, in their great London houses along the river, some of the finest collections ever to be assembled in these islands. Cultural ties, almost invariably interwoven with diplomatic negotiations, bound England to the Continent for the first time since the Reformation. The fabric of this court civilisation rested on the peace which James I sought to establish. It is a constant theme in verse and masques, in the reign of King James and, even more, during the years of Charles I's personal government, that Peace, 'the beautiful'st of things', provided that halcyon prosperous condition, when 'Olive Branches stand for Bayes' and all the arts could flourish. Just before the King's accession, Rubens, describing the persistence with which the Prince of Wales had asked for his *Self-portrait* (No.15), called him 'the greatest amateur of painting among the princes of the world' (Magurn, p.101).

SIR PETER PAUL RUBENS
(1577–1640)

15. **Portrait of the Artist**
Oil on panel: 33¾ × 24½ in. Signed and dated:
*Petrus Paullus Rubens/se ipsum expressit/A. D
MDCXXIII/Ætatis Suæ XXXV*
Her Majesty The Queen
Rubens had returned from Italy to his native Antwerp in the autumn of 1608; on 23 September 1609 he was appointed court painter to the Regents of the Netherlands, the Archdukes Albert and Isabella, with whom friendly diplomatic links were established at the English court. By 1616 Rubens was in touch with Sir Dudley Carleton and it was through transactions with Carleton in 1618 that an important group of pictures by Rubens became available to English collectors. George Gage (see No.8) was closely involved in these negotiations. In 1621 Rubens provided a picture for the Prince of Wales's gallery and expressed his willingness, in a famous letter of 13 September,'to receive the honour of their commands; and regarding the hall in the New Palace [i.e., the Banqueting House], I confess that I am, by natural instinct, better fitted to execute very large works than small curiosities' (Magurn, p.46). The picture for the Prince was apparently a Hunt, but it was thought to be 'a peece scarse touched by his own hand' and the Prince refused to place it in his gallery. Perhaps partly as a substitute, negotiations were put in hand early in 1623 for Rubens to paint 'his owne Pourtrait, to be placed in the Princes Gallery'. Writing on 10 January 1625 Rubens described how the Prince had asked for his portrait: 'il ne me sembloit convenable d'envoyer mon pour-

traict à un prince de telle qualité mais il forza ma modestie' (Sainsbury, p.64; Magurn, pp.101–2).
The portrait was in the Prince of Wales's collection at St. James's. It hung later at Whitehall, in a little room between the Drawing-Room and the Long Gallery, in company with *Self-portraits* by Mytens and Van Dyck.

PAUL VAN SOMER (c.1576–1621/2)

16. **Elizabeth Talbot, Countess of Kent
(1581–1651)**
Oil on panel: 45 × 32¼ in., repr. on p.24
The Tate Gallery, London
Van Somer, a native of Antwerp who had worked in Leiden, The Hague and Brussels, was in London by December 1616 and was much patronised by the Crown for whom he produced a number of official portraits; he was probably a favourite with Anne of Denmark. No.16 was in the collection of Charles I and is a good example of Van Somer's style: richer if perhaps less sensitive than Mytens (to whom he must have been a serious rival for a short but vital period), but in the same Netherlandish manner.
Probably painted c.1618–20. Daughter and co-heiress of the 7th Earl of Shrewsbury, Elizabeth Talbot married Henry Grey, 8th Earl of Kent, in 1601. She was an older sister of Lady Arundel.

15

16

18

17

DANIEL MYTENS (*c.*1590–1647)

17. **Portrait of the Artist**
    Oil on panel: 21½ × 17 in.
    Sir James Fergusson of Kilkerran, Bt.
    Mytens, who had been born in Delft and was
influenced by such portrait-painters as Miereveld
and Ravesteyn, was in London in 1618, when he had
gained the patronage of the Earls of Arundel (see
No.1) and Southampton (No.4) and was hoping
to be employed by the Prince of Wales. James I
granted him in 1624 an annual pension and the new
King in 1625 appointed him one of his official
'picture-drawers of our Chamber in ordinarie' for
life. He probably left London in 1634 and until the
arrival of Van Dyck in 1632 had been the most successful and distinguished portrait-painter at court,
producing for Charles I a succession of official royal
portraits. To the solidity of form and fine technique
which he had acquired in his years of training in
Holland, Mytens added a grave and sensitive mood
and a grandeur in design which at first may have

owed something to the full-length tradition at the English court, but which, in his late masterpieces (e.g., Nos.22, 23), have a swagger which no conventional Dutch portrait-painter surpassed. Only Van Dyck's mature court style could make such portraits seem out of date. They are the most accomplished essays in the Anglo-Netherlandish style in which Mytens and his contemporaries worked: a style which, with the manner introduced by Van Dyck, form the two stylistic poles to which painting in England in the age of Charles I can be related (Millar, *Tudor, Stuart*, pp.84–89; Ter Kuile).

No.17 was probably painted *c*.1630. It is a less formally composed statement than the *Self-portrait* which was painted for the King and is still in the royal collection (Ter Kuile, p.83 (No.72)).

18. Charles I when Prince of Wales
Oil on canvas: 71 × 56 in.
From the Collection at Parham, Pulborough, Sussex
Painted in 1623, probably soon after the return of the Prince from Spain on 3 October. Mytens was paid £30 on 9 October for a full-length of the Prince which was delivered to the Spanish ambassador. This could have been No.18, or the other full-length, now in the royal collection, painted in that year (Millar, *Tudor, Stuart*, No.117). It is perhaps the most sensitive of Mytens's portraits of the King before his accession and is a good example of the restrained distinction of Mytens's style in the early 1620s (Ter Kuile, pp.53–54 (No.19)).

19. Martha Cranfield, Countess of Monmouth (1601–77)
Oil on canvas: 84 × 50¾ in., repr. on p.26
The Lord Sackville
Probably painted *c*.1620, the year in which the sitter married Henry Carey, 2nd Earl of Monmouth. Her father, Lionel Cranfield, 1st Earl of Middlesex, was one of Mytens's most generous patrons; of the two full-lengths of him by Mytens at Knole, one is apparently dated 1620. No.19 is close in design to the formal full-length Jacobean style of Gheeraedts or of the painter of the magnificent full-lengths which have been attributed to William Larkin (R. Strong in *The Elizabethan Image*, Tate Gallery (1969–70), especially Nos.128–30, 133–9). But there is with Mytens a new solidity of form, and an unassuming humanity in character. It is fruitful to compare Mytens's image with that created by Van Dyck of the same sitter some fifteen years later (No.95).

20. Lady Mary Feilding, later Duchess of Hamilton (1613–38)
Oil on canvas: 27½ × 22½ in. Dated: *Ætatis. suæ: 9. a° 1622*. Recorded in at least one of the inventories of her husband's pictures in the 1640s: 'One picture of my lady, to the middle, in a ruffe, with a feather in her heade of Mittens', repr. on p.26
The Duke of Hamilton and Brandon
Daughter of the 1st Earl of Denbigh and niece of the Duke of Buckingham. 'A most affectionate and dutiful wife', she was Lady of the Bedchamber to Henrietta Maria.

A good example of Mytens's use, in the painted oval, of a favourite device of painters working in the Anglo-Netherlandish style; the modelling is broader and the atmosphere richer than in comparable portraits by Johnson or Gheeraedts and the mood is close to Priwitzer (Ter Kuile, p.67 (No.44)).

21. Sir Henry Hobart (d.1625)
Oil on canvas: 51¾ × 41 in., repr. on p.26
The National Trust (Blickling Hall)
Painted in 1624: part-payment for the portrait is recorded in the sitter's accounts under 22 December of that year. Sir Henry was the builder of Blickling and Lord Chief Justice of the Common Pleas: 'a most learned, prudent, grave and religious judge'. It is one of Mytens's most sensitive portraits and a distinguished example of the standard formula for legal or semi-official portraits: a tradition taken up by Johnson, Lely and a number of lesser painters (Ter Kuile, p.72 (No.55)).

22. George Villiers, 1st Duke of Buckingham (1592–1628)
Oil on canvas: 94½ × 52 in. originally, to which have been added *c*.5 in. at the top and *c*.3 in. at the bottom. Signed and dated: *D.Miitens/f.ᵗ a.° 1626*, repr. on p.27
The Duke of Grafton
One of Mytens's most elegant full-lengths, of which a number of versions are recorded. It was painted for Charles I and placed in the Bear Gallery at Whitehall. Sold for £25 in 1651, it was recovered at the Restoration, but apparently thereafter given away by Charles II to the Duchess of Cleveland or the Earl of Arlington.

The little piece of perspective hanging in the background is by Hendrick van Steenwyck; during the Interregnum a dealer was offered £5 for it by itself. Steenwyck (see No.131) was frequently employed to paint complete perspective backgrounds

19

20

21

against which portrait-painters such as Mytens could place their sitters (Ter Kuile, pp.50–51 (No.11)).

23. James Hamilton, 3rd Marquess and 1st Duke of Hamilton (1606–49)

Oil on canvas: $87 \times 55\frac{1}{2}$ in. Signed and dated: *D: Mytens fe.^t anno 1629*. Recorded in an inventory of the Duke's pictures in the 1640s: 'One picture of my lords, standinge at length, with his hatt in his hande of Mittens', repr. p.28
The Duke of Hamilton and Brandon

The Duke was prominent among the collectors of the time. He was closely involved with the King's collection, was given important pictures by the King, and brought pictures back for him from Germany; his brother-in-law, Lord Feilding, was Ambassador to Venice and secured good pictures for him. The Duke was less successful as a politician and a soldier and ended his life on the scaffold a few days after his master.

No.23 is Mytens's masterpiece: certainly the most distinguished full-length painted at the Stuart court before the arrival of Van Dyck and worthy to hang beside any comparable full-length painted up to that time by any court painter in northern Europe. The silver-grey tonality is quite personal and the accessories are laid out with unusual, almost De Champaigne-like, lucidity. The background appears to be partly unfinished (Ter Kuile, pp.53–72 (No.53)).

MARCUS GHEERAEDTS the YOUNGER (*c.*1561–1635)

24. Portrait of a Woman

Oil on panel: 44×36 in.
The Duke of Norfolk

Probably painted *c.*1625, No.24, with its tender mood, delicate handling and sensitive colour, can be confidently attributed to the last phase of Gheeraedts's career; it could be compared with his portraits of Mrs Hoskins (1629), Lady Fanshawe and two portraits at Adare, of which one was sold at Christie's, 17 March 1972 (72). This quiet, unruffled style is beginning to look slightly old-fashioned.

If the sitter, who is clearly *enceinte*, is a member of the Constable family, she could be Anne, daughter of Sir William Roper, who married Sir Philip Constable of Everingham. Her first two children were born in 1618 and 1619; successive births took place until 1630.

22

25. **Richard Tomlins (1564(?)–1650(?))**

Oil on panel: 44 × 33 in. Signed: *Marcus gheeradts/fecit*; and inscribed: *Anno Doi 1628./ Ætatis suæ 64.* The sitter's name is inscribed, probably by the painter, above the coat of arms.

The Curators of the Bodleian Library, Oxford

By this late period in his career Gheeraedts had lost the patronage of the court and was probably finding his patrons principally among scholars and country gentlemen. Richard Tomlins, who lived in Westminster and Richmond, had founded the Anatomy lecture at the University in 1623. The friendly and unpretentious mood of the portrait and its comparatively two-dimensional presentation make it seem old-fashioned, but it represents a style in which painters outside the court circle, in the City and in the provinces, worked until the 1640s: a style which was almost unaffected by Mytens and still less by Van Dyck and in which an almost neo-Elizabethan spirit is kept alive (O. Millar in *Burl. Mag.*, CV (1963), p.538; R. Strong, *The English Icon* (1969), p.275).

26. **Charles Hoskins (1603–1657)**

Oil on panel: 26 × 20¾ in. Inscribed by the painter in his distinctive script: *Æ.26./An.º 1629.*

Private Collection

Painted in the same year as the larger, signed and dated, portrait of his wife, Ann Hale. No later portraits by Gheeraedts are known. The use of the painted oval provokes comparison with Cornelius Johnson, who may have been associated early in his career with Gheeraedts; but the older painter draws his sitter more frontally and sets him in space with less conviction than Johnson and does not create around him the richer atmosphere of Johnson in his maturity (O. Millar in *Burl. Mag.*, vol. CV (1963), pp.538–41; R. Strong, *The English Icon* (1969), p.287).

Sir Nathaniel Bacon (1583(?)–1627)

27. **Portrait of the Artist**

Oil on canvas: 81¼ × 60½ in., repr. on p.31
From the Gorhambury Collection by permission of the Earl of Verulam

A country gentleman, of Culford in Suffolk, grandson of Sir Nicholas Bacon, son of Sir Nicholas Bacon of Redgrave, and perhaps the most competent

25

26

English amateur painter of the seventeenth century. He painted a number of *Self-portraits*, of which this is the most ambitious and must have been painted not long before the coronation of Charles I at which Nathaniel Bacon was created Knight of the Bath. 'Cunning in drawing, and the knowledge in the verie art of painting' had for long been held as one of a fully educated gentleman's accomplishments. To Henry Peacham, in the *Compleat Gentleman* (1622), painting was one of the 'generous Practices of youth'. He held that among England's noble amateurs none surpassed 'Master Nathaniel Bacon of Broom in Suffolk . . . not inferiour in my judgment to our skilfullest Masters'. The accessories in No.27 illustrate the breadth of the sitter's interests: the painter's palette (which also decorates his monument in Culford church) hanging between his sword and a little picture of Minerva; books, a drawing in his hand and a large folio open at a map of Northern Europe. Bacon was on his way to the Low Countries in 1613 and it is significant that his portraits are in the Anglo-Netherlandish manner and have points of contact with Mytens. He was asked by the Countess of Bedford to help her with her garden and pursuing pictures: 'whos judgement is so extraordinary good as I know noone can better tell what is worth the haveing'. He also painted still-lifes in the Netherlandish manner: an inventory (1650) of the pictures at Culford Hall includes, on the great stairs and in the gallery, 'Ten Great peeces in Wainscoate of fish and fowle &c done by Sʳ: Nath: Bacon' (*The Private Correspondence of Jane Lady Cornwallis* (1842), pp.50–51).

JOHAN PRIWITZER (*fl.*1626–35)

28. **William, Lord Russell, later 5th Earl and 1st Duke of Bedford (1613–1700) with a Dwarf**
Oil on canvas: 83 × 49 in. Signed: [*I*] *HANNES PRIWIZER DE HVN/[G]ARIA FACIEBAT*; dated (twice) 1627 and inscribed with the ages (14 and 32) of the sitters.
His Grace the Duke of Bedford and the Trustees of the Bedford Settled Estates

29. **Francis Russell (1619–41)**
Oil on panel: 26 × 20 in. Inscribed: *ÆTATIS SVÆ 8* and dated: *ANNO 1627*; inscribed, perhaps slightly later, with the sitter's name.
His Grace the Duke of Bedford and the Trustees of the Bedford Settled Estates

30. **Lady Diana Russell (1622–95)**
Oil on panel: 26 × 20 in. Inscribed: *ATATIS SVÆ 5* and dated: *ANNO 1627*; inscribed, perhaps slightly later, with the sitter's name.
Diana Russell married in 1642 Francis Newport, later Viscount Newport and Earl of Bradford, who was a discerning collector of pictures.
His Grace the Duke of Bedford and the Trustees of the Bedford Settled Estates
Priwitzer is an exceedingly obscure painter who was mentioned as being in London in documents dated March 1627 and July 1635; he appears to have been in Spain in 1647 and may have been born in Italy. His only documented works are the set of six portraits of children of the 4th Earl of Bedford, of which two are shown here, and the full-length of the eldest son in the robes of the Bath. One of the smaller portraits is dated 1626. Lord Russell was one of the Knights of the Bath created at the coronation of Charles I; he is later to be seen in Van Dyck's great portrait (No.100) and was painted with equal splendour, in his Garter robes, by Lely and Kneller. Priwitzer's style has obvious affinities with Mytens and, to a lesser extent, Cornelius Johnson; his touch is, however, lighter and his colour set in a higher key; and he endows his sitters with a livelier spirit. His grasp of perspective and the full-length is less assured than Mytens (e.g., in No.22). (Whinney and Millar, p.75).

CORNELIUS JOHNSON (1593–1661)

31. **Sir Alexander Temple (1583–1629)**
Oil on panel: 26 × 20 in. Signed and dated: *C.J./fecit/1620* and inscribed: *Aetatis Suae/37*
The Viscount Cobham
Johnson's earliest portraits (the earliest known are dated 1617) are close in feeling, and even in quality, to Marcus Gheeraedts, and he even seems to have used at this early period a distinctive form of script as Gheeraedts was doing; he may well have been partly trained by him. Johnson's parents had fled from Antwerp during the religious persecutions of the previous century and he had been born in London. His style and circumstances were alike closely involved with the families of artists and craftsmen who belonged to the Dutch Reformed Church in Austin Friars: the Olivers, Colts and De Critzes as well as the Gheeraedts family. In No.31 the surface is more opaque and the texture a little richer than in a comparable portrait by Gheeraedts, and the sitter is not very comfortably placed within

27

28

29

30

31

32   33   34

the painted oval of which Johnson made constant use.

A replica of No.31, formerly at Northwick Park, is now in the Mellon collection.

32. John Raymond (d.1635)

Oil on panel: $30\frac{1}{4} \times 24$ in. Signed and dated:
C.J. Fecit/1627
S. P. St. Clere Raymond, Esq.

John Raymond acquired the Belchamp estate near Sudbury in 1611. The portrait, compared with No.31, shows that Johnson had by now mastered the painted oval; it represents the point at which Johnson's style and presentation come closest to Mytens although his handling is more delicate and less broad than Mytens and his sense of character rather gentler.

33. Charles de l'Aubespine, Marquis de Châteauneuf-sur-Cher (d.1653)

Oil on panel: $30\frac{3}{4} \times 24\frac{1}{4}$ in. Signed and dated:
CJ Fecit/1629
The Dowager Viscountess Galway

The sitter arrived as French ambassador in London in July 1629, and was hostile to Rubens when the painter was working for peace with Spain; he was disgraced in 1633. In No.33 he is wearing the ribbon of the Saint-Esprit; the collar of the Order and the collar of Saint-Michel surround his arms.

The portrait is in its original black frame of the type much favoured at this period; and the sitter's identity is recorded on the frame, on the original

cartellino of a type which was more normally, in the great collections of the time, painted on the canvas itself.

34. Portrait of a Woman

Oil on panel: $16\frac{5}{8} \times 12\frac{5}{8}$ in. Signed and dated:
C.J. fecit–/1630
The Duke of Hamilton and Brandon

Formerly described as a portrait of the Queen of Bohemia, No.34 is an example of the small scale on which Johnson occasionally worked, half-way between the miniature and the life-size scale.

35. Sir Thomas Hanmer (1612–78)

Oil on canvas: $30\frac{1}{2} \times 24\frac{1}{2}$ in. Signed and dated:
C.J. fecit/1631, repr. on p.34
The National Museum of Wales, Cardiff

A comparison between Johnson's portrait and Van Dyck's later portrait (No.103) of Sir Thomas demonstrates the radical transformation wrought by Van Dyck in the development of the British portrait.

36. Anne Leake, Lady Hobart (d.1684)

Oil on canvas: 30×25 in. Signed and dated:
C.J fecit/1632
E. R. Verney, Esq.

37. Anne Uvedale, Mrs. Henslowe (d.1639)

Oil on canvas: $31\frac{3}{8} \times 25\frac{1}{2}$ in. Signed and dated:
Cornelius Jonson–/fecit 1635
E. R. Verney, Esq.

Anne Uvedale, who married Mr Henslowe in

37

1635, and Anne Leake, a cousin of Sir Ralph Verney, were close friends of the Verney family. The latter—'Sweet Nan'—married Sir Nathaniel Hobart, son of Sir Henry (No.21).

The two portraits were perhaps conceived as pendants: Lady Hobart in furs perhaps personifying Winter and Mrs Henslowe as a shepherdess with flowers in her hair. As personifications of Winter and Spring there are close contacts with Hollar's prints of the Seasons (Nos.72, 73). The portrait of Mrs Henslowe is close in mood to the Arcadian portraits by such painters as Honthorst and Moreelse, of which examples were in Charles I's collection; but his portraits for the Verney family (he painted Sir Ralph in 1634) illustrate the circles in which Johnson found his patrons during the 1630s, when he seems to have found the court atmosphere increasingly uncongenial, although he painted a handful of royal portraits, had been sworn in as one of the King's 'Picture Drawers' in 1632 and was still among the King's servants in 1641.

35

38. **The Family of Arthur, Lord Capel (1604–49)**

Oil on canvas: 63 × 102 in. There are remains of a signature near the damaged area on the right. The picture passed by descent in the family of the Earls of Essex at Cassiobury; it was last sold at Christie's, 13 March 1970 (99), when it was acquired for the National Portrait Gallery.

The National Portrait Gallery, London

Painted c.1639. Arthur Capel, a devoted royalist who died on the scaffold on 9 March 1649, married in 1627 Elizabeth, heiress of Charles Morrison of Cassiobury. Assuming that the child on the mother's knee is a boy, the children are presumably Arthur (1632–83), later 1st Earl of Essex, Charles (d.1657), Henry (1638–96), later Lord Capel of Tewkesbury, Elizabeth (1633–78), later Countess of Carnarvon, and Mary (1630–1715), later Duchess of Beaufort. The design reflects the influence of Van Dyck on Johnson in the 1630s: in the rather clumsy elegance of the individual portraits, in the elaborate background and in the attempt, full of charm if not wholly successful, to compose a baroque group-portrait. In this context the principal influence was perhaps Van Dyck's 'Great Piece' of the King and Queen with their two eldest children, painted by Van Dyck in 1632 and then hanging at Whitehall in the Long Gallery towards the Orchard. The motive of the daughter presenting flowers to the infant could have been suggested to Johnson by the group of the Buckingham family, painted by Honthorst for Charles I in 1628 and also hanging at Whitehall. The gardens behind are thought to be those at Little Hadham, Lord Capel's seat, and the flowers are significant. Mary Capel became a famous horticulturist and Henry Capel established an important garden at Kew.

Rubens in London

On 6 June 1629 Rubens had an audience of Charles I at Greenwich. He had crossed over from Dunkirk the day before. He came, not as a painter, but as a special envoy empowered by the Archduchess Isabella and her nephew, the King of Spain, to work for a truce which could precede formal negotiations between ambassadors for a treaty of peace between England and Spain. Rubens was knighted by the King at Whitehall on 3 March 1630. The peace was proclaimed on 15 December and in the patent which Charles I sent over to Rubens he praised his skill in restoring a good understanding between the two kingdoms.

While he was in London Rubens also characteristically found time to paint. He produced a number of portraits, the *Landscape with St. George and the Dragon* and the great allegory, now in the National Gallery, which he gave to the King and which was described in the King's catalogue as 'an Emblin wherein the differrencs and ensuencees betweene peace and wars is Shewed' (Van der Doort, p.4). His work had appealed to the King for many years (see No.15) and his reputation stood very high with English connoisseurs and travellers. In 1621 an Englishman, admiring his new ceiling paintings in the Jesuit Church at Antwerp, had described him as 'ye master workeman of ye world'; and in the autumn of the same year Rubens mentions his willingness to receive commands concerning the Banqueting House at Whitehall from King James and the Prince of Wales. The old Banqueting House at Whitehall had been burnt to the ground on 12 January 1619, but work had begun by June of the same year in Inigo Jones's new building. By 25 April 1621 a Garter procession and feast were held there and Ben Jonson and Inigo's *Masque of Augurs* was performed there on Twelfth Night, 1622. The expenditure on the entire building, submitted in 1633, concludes with 'a Ceeling divided into a Frett made of Great Cornishes inriched wth carvings with painting'. The nine huge canvases, painted by Rubens in Antwerp after discussion and the submission of sketches, were on their way to London in the autumn of 1635. In June 1638 Rubens received the full payment of £3000 and a golden chain. The performance of masques in the Banqueting House was suspended because of the harm that could come to 'the pieces of painting of great value, figuring the acts of King James of happy memory', from the smoke of the many lights below.

The significance of the Whitehall ceiling can hardly be over-estimated. It is the crowning glory of the 'faire' Palladian building in which Jones displayed the architectural ideals which revolutionised the development of English architecture. It is a paradox that the great painter of the Counter-Reformation should have produced for a heretic sovereign the only one of his decorative schemes which survives in its original setting. Evolved through a series of sketches of exceptional beauty and vigour, the ceiling shows Rubens at the height of his powers, displaying for the early Stuarts, as he had done for Gonzagas, Bourbons, Medici and Habsburgs, his knowledge of classical allegory and his powers as a designer on a huge scale, steeped in the Venetian tradition—in Titian, Veronese and Tintoretto—which particularly delighted the King. The iconographical themes of the ceiling—'the portraictures of *King James* in several relations with all Imaginary similitude of Him, tending towards

Eternity'—express some of the ideas which were essential to the culture of the Jacobean and Caroline court. On the ceiling, as in much contemporary writing and especially in the masques with which the building was so closely associated, there is an emphasis on the Union of the Crowns, the supremacy of Wisdom, the Divine Authority of the King, the King as the source of Justice and the supporter of Religion; on the horrors of Discord and, above all, on the blessings of Concord and Peace, under whose gentle reign the arts could flourish. This theme was especially dear to Rubens. 'This island, for example', he wrote to Dupuy on 8 August 1629, 'seems to me to be a spectacle worthy of the interest of every gentleman, not only for the beauty of the countryside and the charm of the nation; not only for the splendour of the outward culture, which seems to be extreme, as of a people rich and happy in the lap of peace, but also for the incredible quantity of excellent pictures, statues and ancient inscriptions which are to be found in this Court' (Magurn, p.320) (see particularly P. Palme, *Triumph of Peace* (1957); O. Millar, *Rubens: The Whitehall Ceiling* (1958); J. Held in *Burl. Mag.*, vol., CXII (1970), pp.274–81).

39. **The Apotheosis of James I**
Oil on panel: $37\frac{3}{8} \times 24\frac{7}{8}$ in., repr. on p.40
Mrs Humphrey Brand
Although Rubens had expressed as early as 1621 a willingness to serve James I and the Prince of Wales 'regarding the hall in the new palace', there is no evidence that he received a definite commission, or had discussions about the design and iconography of the ceiling, before he came to London in 1629. Nor is there any earlier sketch for the project than No.39, which seems to have been painted at about this period and may have been carried out on a panel used earlier for a sketch for the Henry IV cycle, on which Rubens had begun work by January 1628, but which was abandoned in 1631. There is no evidence for dating No.39, but it may have been painted before Rubens had actually seen the Banqueting House, and when he knew only in general terms what the theme of the ceiling was to be.

In the centre of the panel, which is painted almost entirely in monochrome, is a study for the Apotheosis of James I, perhaps an indication that this had always been intended to be the central iconographical motive of the ceiling; but the panel is unique in Rubens's work in also showing studies for (six) other sections of a decorative scheme on the surface of one sketch. All seven subjects are treated more dramatically, particularly in their steeper perspective, than the relevant parts of the final ceiling. The panel provides an unsurpassed commentary on the workings of Rubens's mind and hand. In the Apotheosis, James I is supported by Justice and sustained by Religion. He is borne upwards to receive a heavenly crown. Above his head Victory (or

Peace) and Wisdom, in the shape of Minerva, hold a wreath of laurel. This design was drawn out within narrower confines in the central sector of the finished ceiling. Between this sketch and the final canvas for the ceiling Rubens painted for Charles I's 'approveing thereof' the *modello* which belonged to the king (Van der Doort, p.91) and of which a copy(?) is in the Hermitage. In the final design the royal robes and regalia are clearly defined.

The panel also contains Rubens's first ideas for the oval canvases which were to occupy the four corners of the ceiling: Bounty and Avarice, Reason and Intemperance, Hercules slaying Envy (or Rebellion) and Wisdom overcoming Ignorance: themes which symbolise the union of Wisdom and Heroic Virtue. The top and bottom of the panel, finally, are filled with sketches for the two friezes of *putti* which, on the ceiling, link these ovals along the longer axis (O. Millar in *Burl. Mag.*, vol. XCVIII (1956), pp.258–67).

40. **The Bounty of James I triumphing over Avarice**
Oil on panel: $21\frac{1}{4} \times 12\frac{3}{16}$ in.
Dr Count Antoine Seilern
On four separate panels Rubens worked out the next stage of his designs for the four oval canvases in the corners of the Whitehall ceiling, for which his first ideas are struck out in the Glynde sketch (No.39). In these sketches the colours are worked out and the figure compositions are set within rectangular limits. The designs tend to become gradually less dramatic and the tensions are slackened further on the final canvas. *Modelli* such as

39

39 (detail)

41

No.40 could perhaps have been submitted to the King for his approval and would certainly have been used in Rubens's studio when the designs were being transferred to the big canvases (Count A. Seilern, *Flemish Paintings and Drawings at 56 Princes Gate* (1955), p.65).

41. **James I**
Oil on panel: 25 × 19 in.
Private Collection
An example of Rubens working out in detail passages from the big compositions on the Whitehall ceiling. No.41 is a study for the figure of James I and an attendant at his side in the second of the two rectangular canvases flanking the Apotheosis. The theme is the Union of the Crowns. The two figures appear very much as in the *modello* in the Hermitage for the whole composition (Oldenbourg, p.334).

42. **Sir Theodore Turquet de Mayerne (1573–1655)**
Oil on canvas: $53\frac{1}{2} \times 42\frac{7}{8}$ in, repr. on p.42
The North Carolina Museum of Art
Mayerne was a celebrated French physician who came to England in 1606; he was Physician to James I, Charles I and their consorts. He was deeply interested in artists' pigments and his notebooks contain valuable references to painters at work in London. No.42 was painted after Rubens's return to Antwerp from London. Rubens sent the portrait over to Mayerne, who acknowledged it in a letter dated 25 March 1631. The frontal pose and the relation between sitter, landscape background and statue (of Aesculapius) in a niche behind, suggest that the portrait influenced William Dobson. The portrait is closely connected with the drawing No.43.

43. **Sir Theodore Turquet de Mayerne (1573–1655)**
Black chalk; washes of ink and water-colour; the head in oil; paper: $12\frac{1}{8} \times 8\frac{5}{8}$ in, repr. on p.42
The Trustees of the British Museum
No.43 is probably a *ricordo* of the portrait painted by Rubens during his visit to London, where he had a number of meetings with Mayerne, and would have been used in Antwerp when Rubens came to paint his principal portrait (No.42) of the physician (Burchard and d'Hulst, No.171).

42

43
44

44   **Thomas Howard, Earl of Arundel
(1585–1646)**
Brush and brown ink, with some carmine;
heightened with white oil-colour; paper:
$18\frac{1}{4} \times 14$ in.
*The Sterling and Francine Clark Art Institute,
Williamstown*

A rapid study for the great three-quarter-
length, now in the Isabella Stewart Gardner
Museum (Oldenbourg, p.288), which was painted
while Rubens was in London. To the same commission can be attached the head and shoulders of the
Earl in the National Portrait Gallery (2391) (Burchard and d'Hulst, No.172).

SIR ANTHONY VAN DYCK (1599–1641)

45. **Inigo Jones (1573–1652)**
Black chalk on paper: $9\frac{5}{8} \times 7\frac{7}{8}$ in. The inscription below records the presentation of the drawing to Lord Burlington by the 3rd Duke of Devonshire, repr. on p.44
The Devonshire Collection, Chatsworth. Lent by the Trustees of the Chatsworth Settlement

Inigo Jones had been described as early as 1606 as one 'through whom there is hope that sculpture, modelling, architecture, painting, acting and all that is praiseworthy in the elegant arts of the ancients, may one day find their way across the Alps into our England'. So richly did he fulfil this promise, as architect, designer and authority on the arts in general, that he occupies an unrivalled place in the history of English taste for his part in bringing continental tastes, knowledge and methods to the English court. His masque drawings show that he had mastered the mechanics of baroque stage-craft, was learned in classical allegory and mythology and could draw with a fluency admired by Van Dyck himself.

No.45 was used as the basis of Van Voerst's engraving of Jones in Van Dyck's *Iconographie* (M.-H., No.72). Principally through the print it became the standard representation of Jones, much copied and adapted in the age of Burlington and William Kent (for an introduction to Jones, see J. Summerson, *Inigo Jones* (1966)).

INIGO JONES (1573–1652)

46-57. **Drawings for 'Salmacida Spolia'**
The masque, by Sir William Davenant, was performed at Whitehall on 21 January 1640, by lords and ladies led by the King and Queen. The last masque performed before the outbreak of the Civil War, its theme is the triumph of Concord who descends to assist Philogenes (the part played by Charles I) in expelling Discord who, 'having already put most of the world into disorder, endeavours to disturb these parts, envying the blessings and tranquillity we have long enjoyed'. The masque contained, therefore, the last statement on this scale of the themes laid out on the ceiling of the Banqueting House (Davenant, *Dramatic Works*, (1872), vol. II, pp. 301–31; R. Strong, *Festival Designs by Inigo Jones* (1967–68), Nos.90–103).
The Devonshire Collection, Chatsworth. Lent by the Trustees of the Chatsworth Settlement

46. **Storm and Tempest**
Pen and brown ink on paper: $7\frac{1}{2} \times 12\frac{1}{8}$ in.
Inscribed: *1 seane for y^e king and queenes masque 1640*
The opening scene: 'as if darkness, confusion and deformity, had possest the world'.

47. **Three Furies**
Pen and brown ink on paper: $11\frac{1}{2} \times 6$ in.
A Fury, snake-haired and brandishing a sable torch, summons up three Furies to spread deceit and discord.

48. **Head-dress for a Fury**
Pen and black ink on paper: $11 \times 7\frac{1}{4}$ in.

49. **A Peaceful Country**
Pen and brown ink on paper: $11\frac{5}{8} \times 7\frac{1}{4}$ in.
The scene changes into a calm and fruitful landscape: 'a country in peace, rich and fruitful. There came breaking out of the heavens a silver chariot, in which sate two persons, the one a woman . . . representing Concord . . . below her sate the good Genius of Great Britain . . .'

45

50. **Three Drawings for the Anti-Masque Entries**
   a. Pen and black ink, washed with grey, on paper: $7\frac{1}{8} \times 4\frac{1}{2}$ in. Inscribed: *Operator*.
   b. Pen and black ink, on paper: $12\frac{3}{16} \times 7\frac{11}{16}$ in. Inscribed: *Tartalia*.
   c. Pen and brown ink, on paper: $12\frac{1}{4} \times 7\frac{3}{4}$ in.
   The drawings are for Wolfgangus Vandergoose, Spagrick, Operator to the invisible Lady; Doctor Tartaglia; and two of the four Grotesques or drollities.

51. **The Way to the Throne of Honour**
   Pen and brown ink on paper: $7\frac{7}{8} \times 11\frac{3}{8}$ in.
   Inscribed: *sceane of mountaines the way to the seat of honour*
   The third scene, 'craggy rocks and inaccessible mountains'; the chorus of the beloved people, led by Concord and the good Genius of Great Britain.

52. **The King as Philogenes**
   Pen and brown ink on paper, corrections in chalk or paint: $11\frac{1}{4} \times 6\frac{1}{2}$ in. Inscribed: *for y^e kinge 1640*
   'The habit of his Majesty and the Masquers was of watchet richly embroidered with silver, long stockings set up of white; their caps silver with scrolls of gold, and plumes of white feathers'.

53. **Design for Masquers (?)**
   Pen and black ink, on paper: $11\frac{3}{4} \times 7\frac{13}{16}$ in.

54. **Design for a Masquer(?)**
   Pen and black ink, washed with grey, on paper: $10\frac{1}{16} \times 6\frac{1}{4}$ in. The flap conceals a variant design for the head-dress.

55. **The Queen, or a Masquer, in Amazonian Habit**
   Pen and brown ink, washed with grey, on paper: $10\frac{1}{2} \times 6\frac{1}{2}$ in.
   The Queen and her ladies were 'in Amazonian habits of carnation, embroidered with silver, with plumed helms, baudrickes with antique swords hanging by their sides'.

56. **A Great City**
   Pen and brown ink on paper: $12\frac{1}{8} \times 16\frac{1}{2}$ in.
   The final scene: magnificent buildings with a bridge over a river. There appeared a cloud, bearing eight personifications of the spheres, and two lesser clouds 'full of music'. These, with a heaven-ful of deities, sang a final chorus to the King and Queen who were by now 'seated under the State': 'All that are harsh, all that are rude, Are by your harmony subdu'd'.

52

55

57. **The Heavens**
   Pen and brown ink, washed with grey, on paper: $11\frac{13}{16} \times 16\frac{1}{4}$ in.

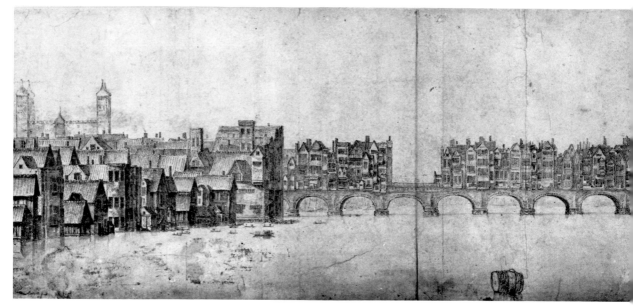

60

58

Sr Francisco Craen Secret: del ord de St Jorge el Ma de Tapisseri.

SIR FRANCIS CRANE

ARTIST UNKNOWN

58. **Sir Francis Crane (d.1636)**
Black and red chalk on paper: $7 \times 5\frac{1}{2}$ in. Inscribed later with the sitter's name and offices.
The Trustees of the British Museum
Drawn c.1625–30. He wears his badge as Secretary of the Order of the Garter. He had been secretary to Charles I as Prince of Wales and was appointed by James I controller of the royal tapestry factory. Crane bought houses at Mortlake in 1619, and in the following year fifty Flemish weavers arrived there. After Crane's death the factory was taken over by the Crown (Hind, p.80).

59

ARTIST UNKNOWN

59. A Prospect of London and the Thames from above Greenwich

Oil on panel: $11\frac{3}{4} \times 36\frac{1}{2}$ in.

The London Museum

Painted, *c.*1620–30, by (almost certainly) a Flemish painter who has not so far been satisfactorily identified. Dr. John Hayes has pointed out that No.59 is the earliest painted view of London seen from a distance; it is also an early example of the popularity of Greenwich, with the first landscape painters in England, among sites near the capital, for the dramatic and atmospheric possibilities which it offered. Charles I owned at least three such landscapes: two by Adriaen van Stalbempt and another by the obscure George Portman who may thus conceivably have painted No.59.

The most prominent distant landmarks are St. Mary Overy and Old St. Paul's; in the middle distance are Deptford and the Isle of Dogs; on the right is Greenwich with the old royal palace. The new Queen's House can be seen, in its uncompleted state, under the hill which leads up to the castle which occupied the site where the Royal Observatory now stands (J. Hayes, *Catalogue of the Oil Paintings in the London Museum* (1970), pp.84–88, No.43).

CLAUDE DE JONGH (*c.*1600–1663)

60. Old London Bridge

Pen with brown ink and grey wash, on paper: 9×39 in. Dated: *London the 18 off April 1627.*

The Guildhall Library and Art Gallery, London

De Jongh was probably a native of Utrecht, where he was recorded as a master in the painters' guild in 1627 and where he was buried; he also had associations with Haarlem. He appears to have visited England on at least four occasions, when he probably made sketches on the spot from which he could work up pictures on his return to Holland. In contrast to the Flemish qualities in No.59 and in, for example, the work of painters such as Keirincx and Wouters, De Jongh brought to England markedly Dutch qualities in his landscape paintings and drawings. His views of London are perhaps the most distinguished and poetic before the age of Canaletto and Samuel Scott; and although he had no perceptable influence in this country he occupies an honourable position in a specifically English tradition of topographical draughtsmanship.

No.60 is a preliminary working drawing preparatory to De Jongh's masterpiece, the *View of Old London Bridge*, signed and dated 1630, at Kenwood. In general appearance the scene is fairly accurately represented, but there are numerous discrepancies in detail, which would not be criticized by a Dutch patron.

61. Old London Bridge

Oil on panel: $25\frac{7}{16} \times 48\frac{13}{16}$ in. Signed and dated: *C d Jongh 1650*.
The Victoria and Albert Museum

A later re-working of the panel of 1630, but without a fresh visit to the scene in the meantime. The technique is now much less rich in texture. Alterations to the original design include the insertion of St. Mary Overy on the right.

62. A Village Street

Pen and brown ink, with brown wash, on paper: $8 \times 11\frac{3}{8}$ in. Dated: *in Aprill 1628*. On the verso is a drawing of two cottages.
The Trustees of the British Museum

The street is certainly English: a rare and delightful glimpse of the rough English scene at this period. The same street occurs in another drawing by De Jongh, dated in the same year, in the Boymans Museum. The drawing illustrates De Jongh working in a contemporary Haarlem style; the build-up of the different elements suggests parallels with Van Goyen at the same period (Croft-Murray, p.382, No.2; J. Hayes, in *Burl. Mag.*, vol. XCVIII (1956), pp.3–11, for De Jongh in general).

WENCESLAUS HOLLAR (1607–77)

63. Richmond

Pen with black ink and colour washes, on paper: $3 \times 7\frac{5}{8}$ in. Signed and dated: *Wentzel Hollar delineavit 1638*, and inscribed *Richmond*.
Her Majesty The Queen

Hollar, who was born in Prague, was working at Cologne when the Earl of Arundel arrived there in 1636 at the head of a mission to the Emperor. The Earl took him into his suite: 'I have one Hollarse wth me, whoe drawes and eches printes in strong water quickely, and wth a pretty spirite'. Hollar accompanied Arundel back to London. By 1644 he had left London for Antwerp, but he returned in 1652. His work as draughtsman and etcher (he produced over 2500 plates) is invaluable to a student of the seventeenth century because it illustrates the whole range of interests in an age when there was a passion for knowledge of all kinds. He helped, above all, to lay the foundations of the topographical tradition in English art in a steady output of plates and drawings. His etchings after Van Dyck's portraits contributed to making the painter's patterns available.

No.63 is a charming example of Hollar's delicate, restrained, but absorbed approach as a topographical draughtsman. The old palace of Richmond, one of the favourite residences of the Tudors, which had been used by Charles I and his brother and was often occupied by Henrietta Maria and her children, is set back in the distance; the foreground is enlivened by a cavalcade of horsemen, with a coach, galloping past a row of houses. The narrative content in Hollar is often peculiarly evocative of the atmosphere of the times in which he lived (Oppé, No.373).

64. The Thames from Westminster

Pen with brown ink, over pencil, on paper: $5\frac{5}{8} \times 15\frac{3}{8}$ in. Signed: *W. Hollar*.
Her Majesty The Queen

The view of the riverside includes the Savoy, Somerset House and, in pencil and unfinished, Old St. Paul's. It is a very good example of Hollar's method as a topographical artist, with picturesque details in the foreground, others left unfinished and in pencil, and the careful topographical statement in the middle distance (Oppé, No.371).

65. Windsor Castle

Pen with black ink and colour washes, on paper: $4\frac{5}{8} \times 10\frac{7}{8}$ in. Inscribed: *Windsor* and *Thamesis fluvius*
Her Majesty The Queen

A view of the castle from the north-east, with Eton College Chapel in the distance, probably drawn c.1640, before the restorations carried out, principally on the north front, by Charles II (Oppé, No.369).

66. Greenwich

Etching (P.977): $5\frac{3}{4} \times 32\frac{5}{8}$ in. Etched in 1637. The view can be compared to No.59, but is taken from a point further to the east. The Queen's House is clearly seen. It had been begun by Jones for Queen Anne of Denmark in 1616, but was not finished until 1637. The decoration of the interior was not complete. The ceiling of the hall was painted by Orazio Gentileschi; more decorative schemes were to be added by Rubens, Jordaens and possibly Van Dyck.
Her Majesty The Queen

67. The Piazza in Covent Garden

Etching (P.909): $5\frac{5}{8} \times 9\frac{7}{8}$ in. Probably etched c.1640. The piazza had been laid out by Jones for the 4th Earl of Bedford in the 1630s. It had been inspired principally by Henry IV's Place des Vosges in Paris and by the church and piazza at Leghorn. The piazza was closed at the west end by St Paul's Church, consecrated in 1638.

Her Majesty The Queen 67

68. Old St Paul's Cathedral: the West End
Etching (P.1020): $8\frac{3}{4} \times 10\frac{1}{2}$ in. Etched (1656) as one of the illustrations to Dugdale's *History of St. Paul's Cathedral* (1658).

By the beginning of the seventeenth century the Cathedral was in a poor state of repair. Restoration was set in hand by William Laud with his customary energy and with Jones as Surveyor. The King undertook personally to finance the restoration of the west end, which was redesigned by Jones as the background for an immense and magnificent portico which was, at the time, the largest to have been built outside Italy: 'a Piece of Architecture, not to be parallell'd in these last Ages of the World'.
Her Majesty The Queen

69. Thomas Howard, Earl of Arundel (1586–1646)
Etching (P.1351/II): $8\frac{7}{8} \times 7\frac{3}{8}$ in. Etched by Hollar, as the Earl's *Coelator*, in 1639, after a portrait by Van Dyck of the Earl with his grandson Thomas.
Her Majesty The Queen

70. Two views of Arundel House
Etchings (P.1034–5), each $3 \times 7\frac{1}{2}$ in. Inscribed: *Adam A: Bierling delin: W Hollar fecit 1646*. The two views show one of the courtyards of Arundel House, lying on the north side of the house, the garden, and the famous galleries (see Nos.1,2) which Arundel had constructed to house his collections.
Her Majesty The Queen

71. Marcus Gheeraedts the Younger (c.1561–1636)
Etching (P.1407/I). $6\frac{3}{8} \times 4\frac{3}{16}$ in. Etched in London in 1644 from a *Self-portrait*, which is now lost, painted in 1627, towards the end of the painter's career, which must have extended from his years of success at the court of Elizabeth I to the early years of Van Dyck's activity in London.
Her Majesty The Queen

72. The Seasons
Set of four etchings (P.610–13). $8\frac{5}{8} \times 6\frac{7}{8}$ in. The plates gave Hollar an opportunity to display his interest in female costume and accessories. In Winter the lady is surrounded by the

72

73

furs, masks and muffs which so intrigued him;
Spring has laid these aside and points to a vase
crammed with flowers.
Her Majesty The Queen

73. **The Seasons**
Set of four etchings (P.606–9): $9\frac{1}{2} \times 7\frac{1}{8}$ in.
Spring and Winter are dated 1643, Summer
and Autumn in the following year. The series
is a more elaborate treatment of the themes, and
related costumes, of the earlier series. Spring is
an artist's proof, lacking the inscription and
with the background of an early seventeenth-
century house and garden, and the lady's muff,
added in pencil. Summer contains a view of
St James's Park, with the canal, Banqueting
House and, in the distance, St Paul's. Autumn
shows a view of the water and terraces at Lord
Arundel's country retreat at Albury. Winter,
perhaps a lady from the *demi-monde* of Blackfriars and the Strand, is seen against Cornhill
and the Old Royal Exchange.
Her Majesty The Queen

74

SIR ANTHONY VAN DYCK (1599–1641)

74. **Nicholas Lanier (1588–1666)**
Oil on canvas: $43\frac{3}{4} \times 34\frac{1}{2}$ in.
*Kunsthistorisches Museum (Gemäldegalerie),
Vienna*
Musician and amateur painter (see No.150). He
was employed as a musician by Henry, Prince of
Wales, composed music for masques and was appointed Master of the King's Music in 1625, a post
in which he was reinstated at the Restoration. He
knew a good deal about pictures, was employed by
Charles I in buying pictures on the Continent, and
bought extensively at the sales of the King's possessions. In 1627 he was in Italy, involved with
Gentileschi's sons in buying pictures for the King.
Richard Symonds stated that he was the lover of
their sister Artemisia. He was obviously a significant
figure in the early history of the art trade in London.
His portrait by Van Dyck, for which there is a
preparatory drawing (No.112) was presumably
painted in Antwerp, *c.*1630–2, before Van Dyck's
arrival in London. It was in the collection of Charles
I (the CR brand was revealed during recent restoration) and hung in the Bear Gallery at Whitehall, next
to Van Dyck's portrait of the Antwerp organist
Liberti. When the King's possessions were sold,
Lanier bought the portrait of himself for £10 on
2 November 1649.

75. **Prince Rupert (1619–82)**
Oil on canvas: $70 \times 37\frac{1}{2}$ in.
*Kunsthistorisches Museum (Gemäldegalerie),
Vienna*
Probably painted in The Hague very early in
1632, with the companion portrait of the Prince's
elder brother Charles Louis (Glück, p.335). The
portraits were never in the English royal collection
(Van Dyck painted the two nephews in one canvas
for Charles I in 1637 when they were in London)
but they would have been instrumental in spreading
a knowledge of Van Dyck's style to Holland.
No.75 is the quintessence of Van Dyck's mature
court style on the eve of his departure for London:
a synthesis between the elegance he had acquired
during his years in Italy and the lucidity and weight
of the finest portraits of his second Flemish period.

Adriaen Hanneman (c.1601–1671)

76. **Portrait of a Man**
Oil on canvas: 29¾ × 24 in. Signed and dated:
Ætatis 34/Anº 163[?2]/Hanneman F; inscribed on a paper held in the sitter's hand:
Deo Patria Tibi.
The Trustees of the Warwick Castle Resettlement
Hanneman, born, and probably trained, in
The Hague, was working in London from 1626 to
c.1637. His earliest portraits are close to Mytens in
mood and handling, but show a richer sense of
atmosphere and movement and a vein of romance,
which reveal perhaps the influence of Venetian
pictures seen in the Caroline collections as much as
that of Van Dyck whose style Hanneman did much
to popularise after his return to Holland. In London
Hanneman was closely associated with the families
of artists and craftsmen descended from the refugees
of the previous century; and his early sitters, such as
No.76 (which was formerly described as 'Macchia-
velli'), were perhaps members of this circle. In
quality it is close to Hanneman's portrait of Peter
Oliver in the royal collection.

76

77. **Cornelius Johnson (1593–1661) with his
Wife and Son**
Oil on canvas: 41⅛ × 54¾ in.
The Rijksmuseum Twenthe, Enschede
No.77, presented to the Museum in 1926, was
recorded by Vertue (*Notebooks*, vol. I, p.61) in the
possession of Johnson's great-nephew, Anthony
Russel; Anthony's grandfather, Nicasius, had
married Johnson's sister Clara. Johnson himself
married Elizabeth Beek or Beke on 16 July 1622;
their son Cornelius, who painted in the manner of
his father, died after 1698. The group was painted
presumably just before Hanneman's departure from
England, c.1637. The design reflects the influence on
Hanneman of such family groups by Van Dyck as
the Digby (No.187) or Porter families: in the
movement within the group, the landscape setting
and the sculptural detail. Johnson was granted on
10 October 1643 a pass to go beyond seas with such
pictures and colours, bedding, household stuff,
pewter and brass as belonged to him. In the group
he appears as a prosperous and authoritative figure,
very much the painter in royal service who was
anxious to be regarded as an armigerous gentleman.
In November 1637 he received a grant of denization
(H. Schneider in *Burl. Mag.*, vol. XLV (1924),
pp.295–9).

77

The Image of The King

The artists who were encouraged to come from the Continent to work at the English court were able, by their training and experience, to produce allegorical themes and images of their royal patrons far more sophisticated than the straightforward portraits painted by their predecessors: themes and images, moreover, which would be seen by the King as in the tradition of the great painters of the past whom he particularly admired. The arrangement of pictures in the Queen's Gallery at Greenwich, for example, was still, in 1639, as it had been in Anne of Denmark's time and was hung entirely with portraits in the tradition of the gallery we see behind Lady Arundel (No.2); but in the Bear Gallery at Whitehall, for instance, fine full-length portraits by Mytens, Honthorst, Van Somer and Miereveld were set off by two magnificent canvases by Rubens, three Van Dycks and the great Charles V by Titian which the King had acquired in Spain (Van der Doort, pp.2–7, 196–8).

The painters from abroad in the King's service placed the quality of his patronage on a truly international plane. They also, in different moods and on varying scales, gave substance to many of the ideals which permeated the court atmosphere. Hendrick Gerritsz. Pot (No.83) and Van Dyck paid tribute, for example, to the King's marriage and, in the birth of the Prince of Wales in 1630, to the union between the lily and the rose (a theme to which Simon Vouet's ceiling for the Queen at Oatlands is dedicated) and to the intertwined martial and peace-loving propensities of his forbears. Van Dyck's portraits of the King celebrate him, often on a scale unprecedented in this country, as the country gentleman, as a devoted family man, living in blissful and fruitful union with his Queen, and as a famous horseman who could play the role of the warrior and hero in an Imperial theme: a theme made up of classical, Venetian and Rubensian elements.

The patterns and images which the painters use in the service of the King are those which the court poets develop and which we hear proclaimed in the court masques. Especially significant in this context is Honthorst's huge *Apollo and Diana* (see Nos.78, 79). The picture could be a record of a moment in a masque. The King and Queen receive the homage of the arts and sciences and, with the Duke of Buckingham, act parts in the design in precisely the same spirit and attire as they would have done in a masque. The canvas, indeed, may actually have been temporarily set up in the Banqueting House, under the ceiling which Rubens was to decorate with a special iconographical programme. The Caravaggesque allegorical style in which Honthorst was working for Charles I in 1628 develops into the decorative style in which he worked for Amalia van Solms in the Huis ten Bosch. Rubens and Van Dyck were finer and subtler painters. Rubens's presentations of the King and Queen as St. George and the captive Princess (No.84), and Van Dyck's sketch for the Garter Procession (No.85), show the King in the role, as the patron and protector of the Order, to which there are copious allusions in the masques. Denham, in his *Cooper's Hill*, actually conjures up the King 'In whose Heroic face I see the Saint Better expressed than in the liveliest paint'. It is significant for the King's tastes as a connoisseur that Rubens's mature technique should still be soaked in reminiscences of Titian and that Van Dyck makes the Garter Knights process in front of a backcloth directly derived from Veronese. Such presentations foster, like the masques and copious Cavalier verse, the same dangerous illusion of perfect peace under a wise and all-providing Sovereign. They could be described in the words which Inigo Jones used to describe the masques in which Van Dyck's patrons so often took part: moving pictures, 'nothing else but pictures with Light and Motion' (see particularly R. Strong, *Van Dyck: Charles I on Horseback* (1972)).

78

80

81

79

82

GERRIT VAN HONTHORST (1590–1628)

78. **Charles I**
Oil on canvas: 30 × 25 in.
The National Portrait Gallery, London
An unexpectedly informal presentation of the King (acquired by the National Portrait Gallery in 1965), painted in London in 1628, almost certainly *ad vivum*. Honthorst was in London from April to December and in London painted for the King the huge canvas, now on the Queen's Staircase at Hampton Court, of *Apollo and Diana*, for which No.79 is a preparatory drawing. In the painting the King appears as Apollo, in an image clearly derived from No.78, the Queen appears as Diana (with Lady Carlisle among her attendants) and the Duke of Buckingham plays the part of Mercury presenting the seven Liberal Arts (National Portrait Gallery, *Annual Report 1965–66*, pp.26–27).

79. **Apollo and Diana**
Black chalk, pen, grey ink and wash, heightened with white, on paper: 15 × 22 $\frac{15}{16}$ in.
The Museum Boymans-van Beuningen, Rotterdam
A preparatory drawing for the huge canvas (see No.78) which Honthorst painted in 1628. At this stage he does not appear to have conceived the

protagonists as portraits, but the basic elements in design and iconography have been established. In the left foreground putti personifying Virtue and Love vanquish Envy and Hate. Honthorst was lavishly rewarded by the King for his services. In the later 1630s the painting was in store in a passage room near the Banqueting House (J. R. Judson, *Gerrit van Honthorst* (The Hague, 1959), pp.112–17, 181–3, 256–7).

80. **Prince Maurice (1620-52)**
Oil on canvas: 20 × 17 in.
The Earl of Bradford
The portrait is closely connected with the figure of the Prince in Honthorst's huge allegory, *Seladon and Astrea*, which he painted for Charles I in 1629 and in which the parts are played by the King and Queen of Bohemia and their children. He received £210 from the King for the picture: 'The King and Queene of Bohemia and their Childeren in manner of Storie', placed in the Gallery at St. James's. It is now in the collection of Prince Ernst August of Hanover (H. Braun, *Gerard und Willem*

van Honthorst (Göttingen, 1966), pp.227–30). There is a similar head of Prince Rupert, likewise related to the big picture, in the Duke of Northumberland's collection.

81. **Portrait of a Boy as a Cupid**
Oil on canvas: 20 × 17 in.
The Earl of Bradford
No.81 should probably be regarded as a companion to No.80, and therefore as associated with *Seladon and Astrea*, although no child in the design fits exactly with it. The child is perhaps Prince Edward (1624–63), the fifth son of the Queen of Bohemia.

82. **Elizabeth, Queen of Bohemia (1596–1662)**
Oil on canvas: 29 × 24 in. Signed and dated 1650
The National Trust (Ashdown House)
The Queen and her family extensively patronised Honthorst in The Hague after their flight from Prague in 1620. He produced a huge number of portraits of the King, Queen and their children;

No.82 is one of the set, now partly dispersed, which was formerly in the collection of the Earl of Craven and is thought to have been formed originally by the Queen's devoted supporter, the 1st Earl of Craven.

HENDRICK GERRITSZ. POT
(c.1585–1657)

83. Charles I, Henrietta Maria and Charles, Prince of Wales
Oil on panel: $18\frac{5}{8} \times 23\frac{1}{2}$ in., repr. on p.55
Her Majesty The Queen

Presumably painted in 1632, when Pot was in London; a single portrait of Charles I, signed and dated 1632 and very close to No.83, is in the Louvre. The Prince of Wales had been born on 29 May 1630. The sprigs of olive held by the child and his mother allude to the peace-making activities of James I; leaves of laurel refer to the martial reputation of the Queen's father, Henry IV of France. This fusion of peace and war in the union between Charles I and his Queen was illustrated by Van Dyck in the same fashion; the same note was struck by Ben Jonson in his masque, *Love's Wel-come . . . at Bolsover*, of 1634.

SIR PETER PAUL RUBENS
(1577–1640)

84. Landscape with St. George and the Dragon
Oil on canvas: $59\frac{1}{2} \times 78\frac{1}{2}$ in.
Her Majesty The Queen

While Rubens was still in London it was reported, in a letter dated 6 March 1630, that he 'hath drawn with his pencil the history of St. George, wherin (if it be possible) he hath exceeded himself; but the picture he hath sent home into Flanders to remain as a monument of his abode and employment here'. It was, however, probably secured for the King by Endymion Porter ('The great St George' by Rubens was recorded by Van der Doort (p.171) in the same passage room as Honthorst's *Apollo and Diana*.)

It is clear, principally from X-ray, evidence during restoration and evidence from two preliminary drawings (Held, pp.117–18; Burchard and d'Hulst, Nos., 145, 146) that Rubens completed the design on a much smaller scale ($c.37\frac{1}{2} \times 51\frac{1}{2}$ in.) and later enlarged it, presumably after his return to Antwerp; there is a much later addition of $c.3$ in. at the bottom.

84

The Saint is almost certainly a romantically conceived portrait of Charles I; the Princess would therefore be a rather plumped-up representation of Henrietta Maria. The buildings in the distance are slightly idealised impressions of buildings which Rubens would have seen in London. The most obviously recognisable are Lambeth Palace and the Church of St. Mary Overy. No.84 was acquired by George IV in 1814.

Sir Anthony van Dyck (1599–1641)

85. **Charles I and the Knights of the Garter in Procession**
   Oil on panel: $11\frac{1}{2} \times 51\frac{7}{8}$ in., made up of two separate panels; on the back of each is the CR brand; repr. on p.58
   The Duke of Rutland
   Le dessein du Roy et tous les Cheveliers, probably painted in 1638, appears on a list of works for which Van Dyck was asking payment from the King. It was certainly retained by the King and is the only surviving evidence, taken with an important passage in Bellori (*Le Vite* . . . (Rome, 1672), pp.262–3), for a scheme apparently submitted to the King through Sir Kenelm Digby's means towards the end of the 1630s. The project was for a set of four tapestries, based on Van Dyck's designs, to be hung in a *gran salone* at Whitehall and illustrating the history and ceremonial of the Garter. Charles I was 'the greatest Increaser of the Honour and Renown of this most Illustrious Order' (E. Ashmole, *The Institution, Laws & Ceremonies of the most noble Order of the Garter* (1672), p.196). No.85 would be the design for, in Bellori's words, 'la Processione de' Cavalieri ne' loro habiti'; Van der Doort (p.158) describes them as 'goeing a Precessioning upon S^t. Georgs day'.
   The Chapters of the Order were, in Charles I's time, normally held at Whitehall. No.85 records fairly accurately the Grand Procession to the Chapel on the Feast of St. George's Day: the group of Gentlemen-at-Arms heralding the King's approach; his train borne by a group of noble youths and his canopy of cloth of gold supported by four gentlemen. In front of the Sovereign walk: a nobleman carrying the Sword of State; the Prelate and Chancellor of the Order; Garter King of Arms, the Register and Black Rod; and the Knights in procession (O. Millar, in *Burl. Mag*, vol. XCVI (1954), pp.39–42).

85 (detail)

85

85

Charles I and the Court of Rome

Charles I owned a number of fine pictures by contemporary Italian painters: the Carracci, Guido Reni, Baglione, Fetti and Caravaggio. He was as anxious to establish links with painters in the south (Guercino and Albani turned down his invitation to come to London) as with the studios in the Netherlands; and he would again have been inspired by the influence of such fellow-collectors as Arundel, Buckingham and the Hamiltons and assisted by diplomats such as Wotton and Carleton. The Queen, as a devout Roman Catholic, was naturally fond of religious pictures, and she was also to some extent involved in establishing in London Orazio Gentileschi (No.119) who had been working at her mother's court in Paris for two years. Gentileschi was given rooms, under Buckingham's auspices, at York House; his most important commission from the Queen was the decoration of the hall of the Queen's House at Greenwich with the nine canvases of Apollo and the Muses, in which he was assisted by his daughter Artemisia and which survive, as a reminder of the kind of pictures Henrietta Maria liked but in a mutilated condition, at Marlborough House. He was the only distinguished decorative painter working at the English court and it is perhaps significant that Van Dyck's *Cupid and Psyche* (No.109) was probably painted after Gentileschi's death and as part of a decorative project at Greenwich. The King also owned a number of pictures by the painter's daughter Artemisia (No.90).

After the election of Maffeo Barberini as Pope Urban VIII in 1623 and the King's marriage to his Catholic consort two years later, efforts were made by the Pope's nephew, Cardinal Francesco Barberini, to draw England closer to the Roman Catholic fold, or at least to encourage the King to look with more favour on his Catholic subjects. Negotiations could be carried out by the Papal agents in London under cover of conversations about art and assisted by presents of pictures. A group of pictures, which was sent to the King and Queen in 1635, included works by Albani, Turchi, Stella and possibly Romanelli. In her chapel at Somerset House the Queen was able to install a fully developed baroque setting for Roman Catholic worship. Cardinal Francesco Barberini was involved in the commission from the Queen to Guido Reni for a large *Bacchus and Ariadne*, destined perhaps to hang at Greenwich; and it was the Cardinal who authorised Bernini to carve in marble in 1636 the bust of the English King which caused the Queen such delight. Nothing perhaps illustrates so clearly the chasm between Court and Country in the 1630s as these communications, so fruitful in the artistic field, between Whitehall and the Vatican. William Prynne attacked the Papal nuncio who attempts to corrupt the chief men at court and 'to seduce the King himself with Pictures, Antiquities, Images & other vanities brought from *Rome*' (M. Levey, *The Later Italian Pictures in the Collection of H.M. The Queen* (1864), pp.10–19; R. Lightbown, loc. cit.).

86

87

Sir Anthony van Dyck
(1599–1641)

86. Charles I in Three Positions
Oil on canvas: $33\frac{1}{4} \times 39\frac{1}{4}$ in., repr. on p.61
Her Majesty The Queen

Probably begun in the second half of 1635. It was despatched to Bernini in Rome, possibly in the care of Thomas Baker (No.239), soon after 17 March 1636 when the King wrote to Bernini, expressing the hope that the sculptor would carve 'il Nostro Ritratto in Marmo, sopra quello che in un Quadro vi manderemo subito'. The portrait, incidentally, remained in Rome in the hands of Bernini's descendants, until 1802; it was eventually bought by George IV in 1822.

Evelyn recorded many years later (in his *Numismata* (1697), p.335) that Bernini had been struck with 'something of funest and unhappy, which the Countenance of that Excellent Prince foreboded' in Van Dyck's penetrating study. That Van Dyck took such pains to paint a complete and most delicately modulated composition, and not to provide merely a record of the King's head from three different view points, was probably owing to his desire (felt also perhaps in painting No.88) to impress the Roman painters and *cognoscenti*. The marble bust had been commissioned by the Queen; Urban VIII and his nephew, Cardinal Francesco Barberini, authorised Bernini to accept the commission. The bust was carved in the summer of 1636 and sent from Rome (its despatch supervised by the Cardinal) in the following spring. It was enthusiastically received by the King and Queen at Oatlands on 17 July 1637: admired 'nott only for the exquisiteness of the worke but the likenesse and nere resemblance it had to the King's countenance'. The Queen rewarded the sculptor with a diamond worth 4000 *scudi*. The bust perished in the fire at Whitehall Palace in 1698.

The design of No.86 had considerable influence on later painters; in working it out Van Dyck appears to have been influenced by Lotto's *Portrait of a Man in Three Positions*, now in Vienna, which then hung (as by Titian) in the Second Privy Lodging Room at Whitehall (Millar, *Tudor, Stuart*, No.146; R. Lightbrown in *The Connoisseur*, vol.CLXIX (1968), pp.217–20).

87. Henrietta Maria
Oil on canvas: $28\frac{1}{4} \times 22\frac{1}{4}$ in., repr. on p.62
Her Majesty The Queen

The Queen's delight at the bust of her husband by Bernini led her to desire a companion bust of herself. She proved, however, reluctant to sit for the portraits needed by Bernini. Late in 1637 she agreed to sit for the portrait in three positions necessary to the sculptor; in fact it was not until the end of August 1638 that three separate portraits of the Queen, and not a three-fold study, were ready for despatch to Rome. Her letter to Bernini, telling him of her desire to have a bust of herself carved on the basis of the portraits which would be sent to him, is dated June 1639; and it appears that the portraits were never despatched to Rome. The frontal presentation is also still in the royal collection, but the study of the Queen's right profile is in the Brooks Art Gallery, Memphis (Millar, *Tudor, Stuart*, No.149; unpublished documentary material generously provided by Mr Ronald Lightbown).

88. Henrietta Maria
Oil on canvas: $39\frac{1}{2} \times 33\frac{1}{4}$ in., repr. on p.64
Private Collection

Probably the finest version of this particular portrait type, and almost certainly the portrait which was being painted in December 1636, according to a despatch from George Con, the Papal agent, to Cardinal Francesco Barberini. It was probably painted as a present to the Cardinal, perhaps partly in gratitude for the part he was playing in supervising the making and despatch of Bernini's bust of the King and for the gift of pictures from the Cardinal which had arrived in January 1636.

It is possible that the gesture of the Queen's hands alludes to her being *enceinte*. Princess Anne (see No.106) was to be born on 17 March 1637. It is interesting to note the change of texture in the paint round the head, which perhaps indicates the area which Van Dyck painted while the sitter was in front of him. The very fine quality throughout the design and the beautifully delicate mood, may, as in No.86, show the extent to which Van Dyck wanted to impress artists in Rome and so important a patron as the Cardinal (O. Millar in *Burl. Mag.*, vol. CXI (1969), pp.417–18).

89

87

ORAZIO GENTILESCHI (1563–1639)

89. **The Penitent Magdalen**
Oil on canvas: $51\frac{1}{2} \times 81$ in.
The Earl of Elgin and Kincardine
Probably soon after his arrival in London, or conceivably just before he came over, Gentileschi appears to have painted for the Duke of Buckingham 'onley a single figeure beeinge a Magdalene', which is thought to be the version of this design which is now in Vienna. Sandrart also records a version painted for the King (*Academie*, ed. A. R. Peltzer (Munich, 1925), p.166), which may be identical with No.89. The design is a fine example of the synthesis of Caravaggesque clarity, Florentine elegance and idiosyncratic narrative which characterises Gentileschi's work in the service of the English court (R.A., *Italian Art and Britain*, (1960), No.29).

90

91

ARTEMISIA GENTILESCHI (1593–1652/53)

90. **Portrait of the Artist as 'La Pittura'**
Oil on canvas: 38 × 29 in. Signed: *A. G. F.*
Her Majesty The Queen

The paintress has depicted herself at work and with the attributes of *La Pittura*: the golden chain (as in No.90), the pendant mask, dishevelled black hair and *drappo cangiante*. The portrait was probably painted before her arrival in England (*c.*1638) and should probably be dated *c.*1630. It certainly belonged to the King. The pictures valued at Hampton Court in October 1649 included both 'Arthemesia gentelisco. done by her selfe' (£20) and 'A Pintura A painteinge: by Arthemesia' (£10). The portrait is a lively illustration of her allegedly raffish character (R. E. Spear, *Caravaggio and his Followers* (Cleveland Museum of Art, 1971), No.29).

GUIDO RENI (1574–1642)

91. **Nessus and Deianira**
Oil on canvas: 102 × 76 in.
Ministère des Affaires Culturelles, Musée du Louvre, Paris

One of the four episodes from the legend of Hercules, painted by Guido for the Duke of Mantua in 1617–21. The four were acquired by Charles I with the Mantuan collection and were hung in the Gallery at St. James's Palace with No.91 and some of the King's finest renaissance and contemporary Italian pictures (Van der Doort, pp.226–8). After the King's execution, 'Herculus 4 peeces &c. done by Guido' were sold for £400 (*Mostra di Guido Reni* (Bologna, 1954), No.16).

Van Dyck in England

After Van Dyck's departure from London early in 1621 the court would have been made aware of the next stages in his career and development by the sight of portraits (e.g., No.74), painted in Flanders and probably brought to London, and by the arrival in 1630 of his *Rinaldo and Armida*. On his return to London in the early spring of 1632 he was warmly welcomed by the King, who knighted him, and gave him an annual pension of £200 and a house at Blackfriars. In the years which he spent in London, until his early death on 9 December 1641, Van Dyck effected a revolution in the development of painting in England: a revolution so dramatic in retrospect that it marks a watershed in the history of English art. His training enabled him to design on a large scale with an assurance which no earlier painter established in England had attempted. He was master of a beautiful technique, a variety of touch and a delicacy of tone far more sophisticated than his predecessors in royal service could display; that these qualities owed so much to his devoted study of Titian, a devotion revived by what he saw in the great collections in London, can only enhance the significance of Van Dyck's presence at the Caroline court. Added to his ability to create such magnificently refined pieces of baroque stagecraft as the royal groups, equestrian portraits and the Pembroke family group at Wilton, Van Dyck had a sensitivity towards the atmosphere of the court which enabled him to capture some of its essential ideas: the concept of the King as hero and warrior, for example, or of the Queen as the inspiration of a neo-platonic cult of courtly love. This same sensitivity perhaps reaches its climax in the refinements of *Cupid and Psyche* (No.109), which may have been painted for Henrietta Maria and may well reflect her tastes; and it gives to his finest portraits a lively, sensitive or melancholy air, and above all an intelligence which, with the transformation wrought by his new range of designs, his supreme elegance and his exquisite feeling for landscape, sets Van Dyck closer in spirit to the great painters of the eighteenth century than to the painters who had earlier worked for Charles I. With Waller, we admire in Van Dyck's portraits 'Not the form alone, and grace, But art and power of a face'.

Although most of Van Dyck's time was taken up with portraits of the royal family and members of their circle at court (the Queen's Catholic and crypto-Catholic friends, for example), some of his finest and most significant portraits were painted of patrons who were fundamentally out of sympathy with the King and were later to move into opposition to him: Bedford, Warwick, Pembroke and the like. And it is interesting to note that the portrait in which Van Dyck most clearly illustrates the cult of Arcadia, in the spirit of the masque, is of the puritanical Lord Wharton, son-in-law of Hampden's friend Arthur Goodwin; and that Thomas Baker, one of the few Englishmen to have met Bernini, was an active parliamentarian during the Civil War.

92

94

95

SIR ANTHONY VAN DYCK
(1599–1641)

92. **Portrait of the Artist with a Sunflower**
Oil on canvas: 24½ × 29½ in.
The Duke of Westminster
The best known version of the portrait of
himself in which Van Dyck introduced the golden
chain, as the symbol worn by *Pittura* (see also
No.90), and the sunflower as an emblem of the art of
painting and as the symbol of the attitude of devotion
to the King and of a special relationship between a
faithful subject and a sovereign who is also his
patron (R. R. Wark, J. Bruyn and J. A. Emmens in
Burl. Mag., vols. XCVIII (1956), pp.53–54, XCIX
(1967), pp.96–97). A plate from this design was
etched in London by Hollar in 1644 with a dedica-
tion to John Evelyn (as *artis pictorae amator &
admirator maximus*) by Hendrick van der Borcht the
younger. Robert Walker's *Self-portrait* (No.160) is
to a considerable extent a reinterpretation of Van
Dyck's theme.

93. **Charles I on Horseback with M. de St.
Antoine in Attendance**
Oil on canvas: 145 × 106¼ in. Dated: 1633.
Her Majesty The Queen; repr. on p.67
Painted to be hung at the end of the Long
Gallery at St. James's Palace ('the king's Matie in
Armoure upon a White Horse . . . in a great large
Carved frame'), where it made a profound impression upon visitors: the painter 'has so skilfully
brought him to life with his brush, that if our eyes
alone were to be believed they would boldly assert
that the king was alive in the portrait, so vivid is its
appearance'. The design can be traced back to
Rubens's equestrian portrait of the Duke of Lerma,
which the King and his companions would have seen
in the Gallery of Philip IV's Casa Real at Valladolid
in 1623. Rubens was perhaps influenced by portraits
of the Roman Emperors on horseback by Giulio
Romano which were among the pictures acquired by
Charles I with the Mantuan collection and were
placed, incidentally, with Titian's Emperors on the
walls of the Long Gallery at St. James's, with a
number of the King's finest Italian renaissance and
modern pictures. No.93 was apparently painted
entirely by Van Dyck. It is wonderfully fresh and
sustained in quality, very delicate in the rendering of
the head and containing a number of *pentimenti*.
Many copies and derivations exist. No.113 is one of

Van Dyck's preparatory drawings for a horse in this
position.
The King, who was a notable horseman, is
attended by the Seigneur de St. Antoine, the 'best
master' in the art of horsemanship. In 1603 he had
been sent over by Henry IV of France with a present
of horses for the King's elder brother. He had remained in the service of the Crown as riding-master
and equerry (Millar, *Tudor, Stuart*, No.143).

94. **Arthur Goodwin (1593?–1643)**
Oil on canvas: 86 × 51½ in. The canvas bears
the date (1639) and an identifying inscription
which are in the script found on the portraits
painted, by Van Dyck and others, for Philip,
4th Baron Wharton, who married in 1627
Goodwin's daughter and heiress, Jane. Most of
the portraits in this series are now in the
Hermitage, but No.94 was given by Sir Robert
Walpole to the 3rd Duke of Devonshire.
*The Devonshire Collection, Chatsworth. Lent by
the Trustees of the Chatsworth Settlement*
The sitter was a close friend of John Hampden
and in the Civil War raised for the parliamentarian
party a regiment of cavalry in his native
Buckinghamshire.

95. **Martha Cranfield, Countess of
Monmouth (1601–77)**
Oil on canvas: 85¾ × 50 in., including a later
addition at the top.
The Earl of Radnor
Probably painted *c.*1635, No.95 makes a
significant contrast with the portrait (No.19) by
Mytens of the same sitter. It reveals the delicately
poised balance of movement, glance and gesture
which Van Dyck brought into the English portrait
and the accessories with which he creates the sitter's
ambience: elements in his style which profoundly
affected the development of English painting and
fascinated his successors. It is portraits such as
Nos.95, 96 which appealed especially to Gainsborough, whose full-lengths are, in turn, the most
distinguished expressions of indebtedness to Van
Dyck. But, even within a very short time of his arrival
in London, Van Dyck's sense of movement, and his
repertory of accessories, were being imitated, with
varying degrees of clumsiness, by the painters whom
he found established here. The curtain, flowering
rose-bush and orange tree, elaborately carved pot,
balustrade and glimpses of landscape were standard
accessories in formal British portraiture from this
point onwards.

96. **Elizabeth Howard, Countess of Peterborough (1603–71)**

Oil on canvas: 91 × 49¼ in., including additions at top (c.4 in.) and bottom (c.2 in.). These additions were presumably made when the portrait, in a sequence of family portraits, was fitted into the panelling of the King's Dining-Room at Drayton by her son, the 2nd Earl of Peterborough. The inscription, identifying the sitter, was probably put on at the same time.
Col. Nigel Stopford Sackville

No.96 is the original of a portrait of which the identity (e.g., in versions at Woburn and Wilton) had until recently been confused, but can be presumed to be established on the testimony of her son. She was 'a Lady of extraordinary beauty', a daughter of William, Lord Howard of Effingham, and married before 7 April 1621 the 1st Earl of Peterborough,

who was also painted by Van Dyck. She held strongly republican sentiments. There is a study by Van Dyck in the British Museum for the upper part of the figure (Vey, No.234, verso) (O. Millar in *Burl. Mag.*, vol. CX (1968), pp.307–8).

97. **William Feilding, 1st Earl of Denbigh (c.1582–1643)**

Oil on canvas: 97½ × 58½ in. Probably painted for his son-in-law, the 1st Duke of Hamilton. In Hamilton inventories of the 1640s it appears as 'Vendick. My Lorde Denbeigh & Jacke', and as 'One peice of my lord denbighs at length, with a fowlinge peece in his hande, and a Blackamore by him of Sʳ. Anthony: Vandyke'. The portrait was presented to the National Gallery by Count Antoine Seilern in 1945.
The Trustees of the National Gallery, London

Feilding's rise in favour at court derived from his marriage, c.1607, to Buckingham's sister Susan. He was in the Prince of Wales's suite in Madrid in

96

97

1623. He was Master of the Great Wardrobe, supported the King in the Civil War as a volunteer in Prince Rupert's Horse and died from wounds received at the attack on Birmingham. In No.97 the Earl is wearing Indian or Hindu jacket and pyjamas, of the type worn by Europeans travelling in India. The costume, the native boy and the parrot in the palm tree allude to the Earl's visit to India and Persia. He returned in the summer of 1633. The portrait should perhaps be compared with Gheeraedts's portrait of Thomas Lee in Irish costume (1594); such a comparison reveals Van Dyck's ability to absorb his sitter in a landscape setting and to build up a subtly romantic evocation of his activities. Among Van Dyck's English portraits, it is remarkable for the rich pigment with which it is painted (G. Martin, *The Flemish School*, National Gallery (1970), pp.52–55 (5633)).

98. Lady Mary Villiers, later Duchess of Richmond (1622–85), with Charles Hamilton, Earl of Arran (d.1640)

Oil on canvas: 83¼ × 52⅞ in. Probably painted

98

for Lady Mary's cousin, the Duchess of Hamilton (see No.20), mother of Lord Arran. In one of the Hamilton inventories, drawn up in the 1640s, it appears as 'One peice of my lady duches of Lenox at length, with a cupid by her of Sʳ. Anthony: Vandyke'.
North Carolina Museum of Art (gift of Mrs Theodore Webb, Noroton, Connecticut)

As the only daughter of the murdered favourite, the 1st Duke of Buckingham, Mary Villiers was brought up, with her brothers, in the royal nursery. No.98 was probably painted on the eve of her marriage in the Royal Closet at Whitehall, on 8 January 1635, to Charles, Lord Herbert. Lord Arran was the only son of her cousin.

The design, with its playful use of the Venus and Cupid motive, is a particularly charming example of the allegorical, mythological guise with which Van Dyck clothed some of his sitters. It is one of his English portraits to be mentioned by Bellori. 'Fece il ritratto della Duchessa di Richemont . . . e questo per la sua unice bellezza, fà restare in dubbio se più meriti l'arte, ò la natura, havendola figurata in forma di Venere; e l'accompagnata l'altro ritratto del figliuolo il Duca di Hamilton tutto ignudo in habito di Amore faretrato, e con l'arco' (*Le Vite . . .* (Rome, 1672), p.262). Lord Herbert died in 1636 and in the following year his widow married the Duke of Richmond.

99. Robert Rich, Earl of Warwick (1587–1658)

Oil on canvas: 83 × 49 in. Inscribed later with the sitter's name, repr. on p.72
The Metropolitan Museum of Art, New York (Jules S. Bache Collection, 1949)

The armour on the shore and the naval engagement in the distance probably allude to the Earl's voyage, 1627–8, in command of a small fleet to attack the Spaniards. The Earl narrowly escaped capture.

As a design No.99 is a good example of the extent to which Van Dyck breaks down the formal limitations within which even Mytens's mature portraits had been confined, and introduced rhythms, movement and allusion which foreshadow the eighteenth century. It is nearer in design and spirit to Reynolds's *Captain Keppel* of 1753 than to Mytens's portrait of Warwick in 1632 (*A Catalogue of Paintings in the Bache Collection* (New York, 1944), No.26; Whinney and Millar, p.71).

99 **101**

100. **George, Lord Digby, later 2nd Earl of Bristol (1612–77) and William, Lord Russell, later 5th Earl and 1st Duke of Bedford (1613–1700)**

Oil on canvas: $99\frac{7}{8} \times 62\frac{3}{4}$ in. Signed or inscribed: *Ant van Dyck Eques P*ᵗ
The Earl Spencer

The young men were related by marriage. Digby was married to Russell's second sister, Anne. The group is one of the most sumptuous of Van Dyck's English works. It contains the rhythms, especially the contrast between static forms and those momentarily poised in action, which he built up within such designs and which were developed more fully in the vast *Pembroke Family* at Wilton and, in embryo, in the *Garter Procession* (No.85). The group stresses by means of attributes, colours and accessories, the contrast between the apparently martial Lord Russell and the learned tastes of Digby who was immersed in literature and philosophy but later became one of the most headstrong, devoted and misguided of the King's supporters. The two young men were together at Magdalen College, Oxford.

101. **Catherine Manners, Duchess of Buckingham (d.1649)**

Oil on canvas: $29\frac{1}{8} \times 22\frac{5}{8}$ in.
The Duke of Rutland

Lady Catherine Manners, daughter of the 6th Earl of Rutland, had married in 1620 the Duke of Buckingham. No.101 must have been painted before her remarriage, in 1635, to the 2nd Earl of Antrim, as she is still palpably mourning the murdered Duke, wearing on her bosom, mounted on a black bow, a miniature of him (see No.209) which is derived from the family group painted by Honthorst in 1628.

No.101 is an indication of the extent to which Van Dyck seems to have been influenced by the gentle mood and unpretentious design of Cornelius Johnson's portraits.

102. **Algernon Percy, 10th Earl of Northumberland (1602–68)**

Oil on canvas: $23\frac{5}{8} \times 53\frac{3}{4}$ in. Noticed by Richard Symonds on 27 December 1652 among the Van Dycks in the Earl's collection at Suffolk House: 'halfe figure holding upon an anchor, & Shipps in prospective'.
The Duke of Northumberland

Probably painted *c*.1638. The Earl had been created K.G. in 1635; in March 1636 he was appointed Captain-General and Governor of the Fleet

102

103

and, on 13 April 1638, Lord High Admiral. These posts are commemorated in Van Dyck's two portraits of him, No.102 and a full-length, leaning on an anchor, which is in the same collection. Both portraits derive from the same sitting and No.102 is apparently the fresher and more convincingly *ad vivum* of the two. The Earl was one of Van Dyck's most important patrons and it was within his political and domestic affiliations that Van Dyck, and later Lely, found some of their most influential patrons.

The unusual shape indicates that it was composed in order to fit into a special position in an interior, probably over a fireplace.

103. **Sir Thomas Hanmer (1612–78)**

Oil on canvas: 42 × 37 in. First recorded by John Evelyn, on 24 January 1683, in the house of Lord Newport: 'some excellent pictures, especially that of Sir Tho: Hanmer of V: Dyke . . . one of the best he ever painted'.
The Earl of Bradford

Sir Thomas was a Page and later Cup-bearer at the court of Charles I. A man of taste and a distinguished horticulturist, he married the sister of Bernini's Mr Baker (No.239). No.103 was probably painted shortly before he set out in the autumn of 1638 on a three year tour of the Continent. It is one of Van Dyck's most delicately poised and brilliantly sustained English portraits, steeped in his recollections of Titian and foreshadowing Gainsborough in the following century. Something of its impact can be gauged by glancing back at Johnson's portrait (No.35) of the same sitter (O. Millar in *Burl. Mag.*, vol. C (1958), p.249).

104. **Philip Herbert, 4th Earl of Pembroke (1584-1650)**

Oil on canvas: $41\frac{1}{2} \times 32\frac{3}{4}$ in.

The National Gallery of Victoria, Melbourne

Probably painted *c*.1628. The Earl holds his wand of office as Lord Chamberlain, a post he held from 1626 to 1641. He and his brother and predecessor, the 3rd Earl, were among the most important and lavish patrons of the arts in their time. They were 'the Most Noble and Incomparable Pair of Brethren' to whom the First Folio was dedicated and the generous patrons of other writers. Wilton House and the pictures that survive from the 4th Earl's collection still combine to illustrate their patronage of Van Dyck, Isaac de Caux, Edward Pierce, Emmanuel de Critz, Jones and John Webb. The Earl deserted the King's cause and the work he undertook on the rebuilding and redecoration of Wilton after the outbreak of the Civil War shows the methods and ideas of the Caroline age carried out by a renegade royalist when the monarchy was in eclipse. The 4th Earl's enlightenment, praised by John Aubrey, counteracts Clarendon's account of his rise in James's affections through pretending 'to no other qualifications than to understand horses and dogs very well.' (U. Hoff, *European Paintings before Eighteen Hundred*, National Gallery of Victoria (1967), pp.38–39).

104

105

105. The Five Eldest Children of Charles I

Oil on canvas: $64\frac{1}{4} \times 78\frac{1}{4}$ in. Signed and dated: *Antony van Dyck Eques Fecit,/1637*. Inscribed with the names and dates of birth of the children. From left to right they are: Mary (1631–60), Princess Royal and later Princess of Orange: James (1633–1701), Duke of York and later James II, Charles (1630–85), Prince of Wales and later Charles II; Elizabeth (1635–50); and Anne (1637–40); repr. on p.75
Her Majesty The Queen

The third of Van Dyck's groups of the royal children, it was painted for Charles I who reduced to £100 Van Dyck's original account of £200 for the picture. It was originally hung, in a carved blue and gilded frame, above the table in the King's Breakfast Chamber at Whitehall. Two drawings and an oil sketch (Nos.106, 116) survive from the preparatory material made by Van Dyck in working on the design, which was obviously, to judge from the large number of copies and derivations, immediately popular.

It illustrates Van Dyck's skill, which he had begun to develop in Genoa, in adapting to small and restless sitters the panoply of official portraiture. The charm of this synthesis was well described by Wilkie: 'the simplicity of inexperience shows them in most engaging contrast with the power of their rank and station, and like the infantas of Velasquez, unite all the demure stateliness of the court, with the perfect artlessness of childhood' (Millar, *Tudor, Stuart*, No.152).

106. Princess Elizabeth (1635–50) and Princess Anne (1637–40)

Oil on canvas: $11\frac{3}{4} \times 16\frac{1}{2}$ in. Inscribed with the sitter's names, the younger wrongly described as Prince Henry (1640–60), later Duke of Gloucester.
Private Collection

A study, almost certainly painted *ad vivum*, of the youngest of the royal children, from which they could be placed on the canvas in No.105 with such slight modifications as the longer hair which escapes from under the cap of the elder child in the painting.

107. Venetia, Lady Digby (1600–33), as Prudence

Oil on canvas: $39\frac{1}{4} \times 31\frac{1}{4}$ in.
Private Collection

106

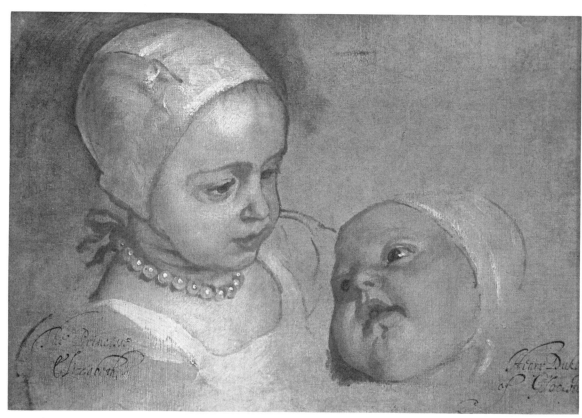

Daughter of Sir Edward Stanley and a celebrated but, in her youth, most imprudent beauty: of 'a most lovely and sweet-turn'd face'; 'a most beautifull desireable creature'. She married Sir Kenelm Digby (see No.187), probably in 1626, and was a devoted wife. He mourned her extravagantly and caused her to be painted 'on a large canvas . . . as Prudence'. Bellori, who was probably given the information on the allegory by Digby himself, describes it in detail and added that Van Dyck was so pleased with the design that he painted a small version of it (*Le Vite* . . . (Rome, 1672), p.261). The best version of the life-size piece is that in the Palazzo Reale in Milan; No.107, which has all the freshness of an original, has the best claim to be regarded as Van Dyck's small replica. The design is the most elaborate example, painted in England, of Van Dyck's allegorical portraiture (Millar, *Tudor, Stuart*, No.179 and Fig.35; *Sir Anthony van Dyck*, Agnew's (168), No.43).

108. **Francis Junius (1589–1677)**

Oil on panel: $9\frac{3}{4} \times 8\frac{1}{4}$ in.

The Curators of the Bodleian Library

Probably painted for the sitter by Van Dyck in 1640. The design was etched by Hollar (P. 1431) in 1659 with that date; on the old frame is inscribed; DNS FRANCISCUS JUNIUS FRANCISCI FILIUS OPERA ANTONII VAN DYKE. The pattern is very close to the small grisaille portraits which Van Dyck had produced in connection with his *Iconography*; and it is significant that Van Dyck had sought Junius's advice in 1636 over an inscription to be placed under an engraving of his portrait of Sir Kenelm Digby.

Junius, a native of Heidelberg, was Librarian to the Earl of Arundel. In 1637 he published his *De Pictura Veterum* (Mrs R. L. Poole, *Catalogue of Portraits* . . . , vol. I (1912), p.61).

109. **Cupid and Psyche**

Oil on canvas: $78\frac{1}{2} \times 75\frac{1}{2}$ in. The original proportions, as given in Charles I's catalogue, were 74×77 in.

Her Majesty The Queen

The moment in the story is the discovery by Cupid of Psyche in the 'dull lethargy' of sleep that overcame her when she opened the box of beauty brought to her from Proserpine at the behest of Venus.

Painted for the King, perhaps as late as 1639–40, and the only one of Van Dyck's subject-pictures, painted at the English court, to survive. It is very sketch-like and spontaneous and may have been left partly unfinished. It was possibly designed to be placed in the Queen's Cabinet at Greenwich, which it was planned to decorate with canvases by Jordaens and Rubens illustrating the legend of Cupid and Psyche, a legend which had, incidentally, formed the theme of a masque by Shakerley Marmion, presented to the King's nephew, Charles Louis, during his visit to London in 1637. In colour and touch, and with its small scale of figures and its poetic melancholy, *Cupid and Psyche* represents a

120

distillation of Titian (far more than of Rubens) and a premonition of an almost rococo spirit which is of significance for such painters as Boucher or Watteau.

Van Dyck's mistress, Margaret Lemon (see No.213), may have been his model for Psyche (Millar, *Tudor, Stuart*, No.166).

Studio of SIR ANTHONY VAN DYCK (1599–1641)

110. William II, Prince of Orange (1626–50), and Mary, Princess Royal (1631–60)
Oil on canvas: 72 × 56 in.
The Rijksmuseum, Amsterdam
The design was Van Dyck's last important commission undertaken for the royal family, and records the marriage of the little couple on 2 May 1641. The Princess wears the large diamond brooch which the Prince gave her on the day after the marriage; the Prince wears the pink costume which had been made for him in London and paid for on 16 May 1641. Van Dyck would therefore have begun work on the design in the middle of May, and before the Prince left London on 3 June. The picture was apparently destined for the Prince's family. It appears in inventories of the Huis ten Bosch from as early as 1654, as by Van Dyck. Since it is now practically certain that the composition was painted in England one may dismiss the recently accumulated hypotheses which involve Hanneman or Lely in its execution. Neither painter was then in England and neither painter's hand can be detected in No.110 which seems, indeed, to be a good late studio piece,

very near Van Dyck himself but perhaps too cold and hard and lacking in delicacy to be regarded as an original. No better version is known at the present time and it is probable that No.110 contains all of Van Dyck that he was capable of producing at this time. He was a dying man and later in the summer of 1641 was obviously finding it difficult to finish two portraits, probably of the Princess, which he had been commissioned to paint (Th. H. Lunsingh Scheurleer in *Oud-Holland*, vol. LXXXIV (The Hague, 1969), pp.29–66, with reference to earlier articles).

Attributed to SIR ANTHONY VAN DYCK (1599–1641)

111. Lucius Cary, 2nd Viscount Falkland (1610–43)
Oil on canvas: 27½ × 22¾ in.
The Devonshire Collection. Lent by the Trustees of the Chatsworth Settlement
Falkland at first supported the Parliamentarian party in the Commons, but later joined the King, serving him as Secretary of State, 1642–3. He fell at the first battle of Newbury. He owes his position in the history of the times mainly to the famous portrait composed in Clarendon's *History* and *Life*. 'That little person and small stature was quickly found to contain a great heart, a courage so keen, and a nature so fearless, that no composition of the strongest limbs, and most harmonious and proportioned presence and strength, ever more disposed any man to the greatest enterprise'. The portrait, like No.101,

110   **111**

is an example of the occasional influence of Cornelius Johnson on the scale and mood of Van Dyck's English portraits. It was probably painted in the late 1630s. The fresh touch and sensitive feeling for character render it difficult to question the traditional attribution to Van Dyck. When Clarendon was building up after the Restoration his historical portrait gallery, it was to No.101 that he directed the painter who was to paint for him a Van Dyckian three-quarter length of his friend.

SIR ANTHONY VAN DYCK (1599–1641)

112. **Nicholas Lanier (1588–1646)**
Black chalk, heightened with white, on blue paper: $15\frac{7}{16} \times 11\frac{3}{16}$ in.
The National Gallery of Scotland
An example of Van Dyck's practice, which he developed in Antwerp and used repeatedly in London, of sketching rapidly the pose of a newly-commissioned portrait, in this instance No.74. On the basis of the approval of such a sketch, the design could be laid out on the canvas to await the first sitting from the patron. In England evidence for such practice is rare before the time of Van Dyck, but Lely, Kneller, Ramsay and Gainsborough, among his successors, imitated his example (Vey, No.203).

113. **Study of a Horse**
Black chalk, heightened with white, on blue paper: $16\frac{7}{8} \times 14\frac{3}{8}$ in.
The Trustees of the British Museum
A study of a horse in the position it takes up in No.93 and therefore probably drawn preparatory to the equestrian portrait of the King, although the design was used by Van Dyck for other sitters (Vey, No.208).

114. **Charles I on Horseback**
Pen and sepia with sepia wash and white heightening, on greenish paper: $11\frac{1}{8} \times 9\frac{3}{8}$ in.
The Trustees of the British Museum
A study, principally for the stance of the horse, in the great equestrian portrait of Charles I, now in the National Gallery (1172); it should be associated with the *modello* in the royal collection. As a pattern the design suggests a synthesis between early English engraved plates of martial sitters, equestrian portraits of Valois Kings and of the King's father-in-law, Henry IV, the traditional image of the King on the Great Seal, and Titian's *Charles V at Muhlberg* (Hind, p.65 (49)).

115. **Charles II when Prince of Wales**
Black chalk, heightened with white, on greenish-grey paper: $13\frac{5}{8} \times 9\frac{5}{8}$ in.
The Trustees of the British Museum
A study for the pose of the Prince, perhaps sketched from life, in the group of the three eldest royal children, painted in 1635, despatched to their aunt, the Duchess of Savoy, and now in the Galleria Sabauda in Turin. In the painting the Prince's left hand is at his side, his right resting on the head of a dog. Van Dyck had difficulty in finishing the group and the King was apparently displeased that he had painted his elder son 'comme on accoustume aux petit enfans' (Vey, No.232).

116. **James II when Duke of York**
Black chalk, heightened with white, on blue paper: $17\frac{11}{16} \times 13\frac{1}{8}$ in.
The Governing Body of Christ Church, Oxford
A study for the figure, and a separate study of the head (both almost certainly from life), of the little boy in the group of the five eldest royal children, painted in 1637 (No.105). (Vey, No.239).

117. **Thomas Howard, Earl of Arundel (1586–1646)**
Black chalk, heightened with white, on grey-green paper: $18\frac{7}{8} \times 14$ in.
The Trustees of the British Museum
Drawn, probably in the late 1630's, possibly in connection with a projected group of the Arundel family, of which No.134 is also evidence (Vey, No.225).

118. **Anne Carr, Countess of Bedford (1615–84)**
Black chalk on light brown paper: $16\frac{1}{2} \times 9\frac{1}{2}$ in.
The Trustees of the British Museum
A rapid sketch for the portrait of the Countess, who was daughter of the Earl of Somerset and married in 1637 William, Lord Russell (No.100). The portrait is one of the set of four Countesses, all at Petworth and probably commissioned by the Earl of Northumberland.

119. **Orazio Gentileschi (1563–1639)**
Black chalk with grey wash; a little pen and sepia; on paper: $9\frac{3}{8} \times 7$ in.
The Trustees of the British Museum
Gentileschi, a native of Pisa, worked in Rome, where he was on friendly terms with Caravaggio. He moved to Paris, *c*.1623–4, and settled in London

114

113

117

119

in 1626 under the protection of the Duke of Buckingham who had met him in Paris in 1625. His influence helped to spread Caravaggism in northern Europe.

No.119 was used by Vorsterman for his engraving in Van Dyck's *Iconographie* (M.-H., No.83). The drawing shows traces of indentation made during transfer to the plate (Vey, No.276).

120. **View of a Town with Trees and Ships**
Watercolour, with pen and ink, on paper:
$7\frac{7}{16} \times 10\frac{7}{16}$ in.; repr. on p.79
The Barber Institute of Fine Arts, University of Birmingham
Generally dated in Van Dyck's English period; few landscape studies survive from before that time in his career. His English watercolours and landscape drawings represent moments of relaxation, as well as the assembling of material for possible use in backgrounds; they are among the earliest spontaneous impressions—certainly the earliest by a great painter—of the English scene (Vey, No.304).

121. **A Wooded Landscape with a High Tree**
Watercolour and body colour on paper:
$7\frac{1}{2} \times 14\frac{1}{4}$ in.
The Devonshire Collection, Chatsworth. Lent by the Trustees of the Chatsworth Settlement
Probably dating from the same period as No.120 (Vey, No.307).

122. **A View of Rye from the North-East**
Pen and brown ink on paper: $7\frac{7}{8} \times 11\frac{9}{16}$ in.
Signed and dated: *Rie del naturale li 27 d'Aug^{to}*
1633 A.vand [ ].
The Pierpont Morgan Library, New York
One of a group of four drawings which are unique in Van Dyck's English *oeuvre* as showing him working at a definite date and in a definite locality; one of them is dated by him 1634. The drawings are in the Flemish tradition and technique of topographical drawing, with, in No.122, an echo of Rubens in the freedom with which the foliage and grasses are drawn in the foreground (Vey, No.288).

123. **A Study of Plants**
Pen and sepia with sepia wash, on paper:
$8\frac{3}{8} \times 12\frac{7}{8}$ in. Signed: *A. Vandijck* and inscribed by the artist with the names of the various plants.
The Trustees of the British Museum
A study from life, possibly dating from the English period. Clumps of foliage of this type appear in the foreground of a number of Van Dyck's compositions (Vey, No.296).

124. **A Country Lane**
Watercolour and body colour on grey paper:
$9\frac{5}{8} \times 15\frac{5}{8}$ in. Inscribed later: *A. Vandyck.*
The Trustees of the British Museum
A group of drawings of this type have not been generally accepted as by Van Dyck, partly because they seem to lack the delicate, nervous quality of line of his finest landscape drawings; but they present a broad and atmospheric impression of the English scene and mark an important stage in the development of the watercolour in England (Hind, p.75 (87)).

123

125. **Portrait of the Artist**
Etching: $9\frac{13}{16} \times 6\frac{1}{4}$ in.
The Trustees of the British Museum
The type probably dates from the eve of Van Dyck's departure from Antwerp for London. The superbly etched unfinished portrait was later adapted by Hendricx for a plate (1645) in the *Iconographie* (M.-H., No.4). This first state illustrates Van Dyck's mastery of the etcher's technique in portraiture. It establishes a method and a mode of presentation which are strikingly modern.

126. **Lucas Vorsterman (1595–1675)**
Etching: $9\frac{3}{4} \times 6\frac{1}{4}$ in.
The Trustees of the British Museum
Particularly associated as an engraver with Rubens in Antwerp and employed to reproduce on copper a number of his master's designs, Vorsterman was, however, very neurotic and went so far, during a mental breakdown, as to threaten Rubens's life. He came to London in 1622, but was back in Antwerp in 1630.

127. **Cornelis van Poelenburgh (1586(?)–1667)**
Engraving after Van Dyck by Pieter de Jode (M.-H., No.35).
The Trustees of the British Museum
The sitter, who specialised in small figure-subjects in the Italianate style (e.g., No.138), which were popular with Charles I, was living in Orchard St., Westminster, in 1639, in a house of which the King paid the rent. Keirincx was a neighbour. The plate for the *Iconographie* (M.-H., No.35) was probably based on a drawing made by Van Dyck on a visit to The Hague in January 1632.

128. **Gerrit van Honthorst (1590–1656)**
Engraving after Van Dyck by Paulus Pontius (M.-H., No.52).
The Trustees of the British Museum
The preliminary drawing by Van Dyck was probably drawn in The Hague in January 1632. The painter had been popular with English collectors since Sir Dudley Carleton had written in 1621 of the 'young man growing into reputation in these parts'; in 1628 he had visited London (see No.78); and his vast output for the Queen of Bohemia and her children would have kept him continuously in the King's mind.

129. **Daniel Mytens (c.1590–1647)**
Engraving after Van Dyck by Paulus Pontius (M.-H., No.56).
The Trustees of the British Museum
The preliminary drawing by Van Dyck (in the Musée Bonnet, Bayonne: Vey, No.264) was probably made in London soon after his arrival. For Mytens, see No.17.

130. **Adriaen van Stalbemt (1580–1662)**
Engraving after Van Dyck by Paulus Pontius (M.-H., No.66).
The Trustees of the British Museum
A Flemish landscape painter who was working for Charles I in London, probably in the 1630s, when he could have sat to Van Dyck for the drawing preparatory to No.130.

131. **Hendrick van Steenwyck (d.1649)**
Engraving after Van Dyck by Paulus Pontius (M.-H., No.67).
The Trustees of the British Museum
Van Dyck's preliminary study (in the Städelsches Kunstinstitut, Frankfurt: Vey, No.268) was presumably drawn in London, where Steenwyck had been recorded in 1617 and where he was active until after 1637. His intricate perspective pieces and night scenes, such as Nos.135–7, fascinated the King and fellow-collectors.

132. **Jan Lievens (1607–74)**
Engraving after Van Dyck by Lucas Vorsterman (M.-H., No.85).
The Trustees of the British Museum
A close friend and associate of Rembrandt in his Leiden years; a picture by him accompanied the two Rembrandts brought back by Sir Robert Kerr (see No.14). He may have paid a visit to London in the 1630s and was in Antwerp, 1635–44, when he came under the influence of Van Dyck.

133. **Mary Ruthven, Lady Van Dyck (d.1645)**
Engraving after Van Dyck by Schelte à Bolswert (M.-H., No.101).
The Trustees of the British Museum
Daughter of Patrick Ruthven, son of the 1st Earl of Gowrie, she married Van Dyck in 1639, to the fury of his mistress, Margaret Lemon (No.213). They had one daughter. Van Dyck died on the day

of her baptism. Lady Van Dyck died soon after her second marriage, to Sir John Pryse. The engraving is based on a painted portrait of which the most familiar version is in the Prado.

PHILIP FRUYTIERS (1610–65)

134. The Family of the Earl of Arundel
Watercolour on paper: 15⅝ × 21¾ in. Signed and dated: *P.H. FRVYTIERS . fect . 1643* and inscribed: *An. VANDYKE Inv.*
Private Collection
Painted in Antwerp and thought to record Van Dyck's design for a large state group of the family on lines comparable in general to the Pembroke family group. The figures of the Earl and his Countess are based on Van Dyckian prototypes. The grand-children appear to have been painted *ad vivum*.

HENDRICK VAN STEENWYCK (*d.*1649)

135. Figures on a Terrace
Oil on copper, circular: 4 11/16 in.
Her Majesty The Queen

136. The Liberation of St. Peter
Oil on copper, circular: 5 in.
Her Majesty The Queen
The pair was certainly in the collection of Charles II and may have belonged to Charles I. Both pieces are fine examples of Steenwyck's intricate sense of design and very fine touch, which clearly delighted Jacobean and Caroline collectors. In No.135 the costumes seem to be of *c.*1625. The imaginary, fairy-tale architectural fantasy is reminiscent of the creations of Vredeman de Vries. No.136 is an example of Steenwyck's favourite subject, which gave him scope in combining the effects of lights at different points of a darkened fantasy in perspective.

137. The Liberation of St. Peter
Oil on copper: 19 × 26 in. Signed: *HENRI.V. STEINICK* and dated 1619.
Her Majesty The Queen
A very fine example of the quality of Steen-wyck's painting of such subjects. The rather limp, elongated figures may be by Steenwyck himself, but are possibly the work of a collaborator.

CORNELIS VAN POELENBURGH (1586(?)–1667)

138. A Nymph and a Satyr Dancing
Oil on panel: 11 × 17 in.
The Earl of Bradford
An example of the type of Italianate Dutch subject-painting which was brought to England by Poelenburgh (see No.127) from Utrecht and was popular with the King and his fellow-collectors. As a style it has affinities, though on a tiny scale, with Honthorst and was perhaps influential on Lely in the small subject-pictures which he painted in his first years in England.

FRANS WOUTERS (1612–1659/60)

139. The Triumph of Bacchus
Oil on panel: 17¼ × 26¾ in.
Sir Gyles Isham, Bt.
Wouters, who had been trained in Antwerp, came to England in 1636, but was back in Antwerp by August 1641; he was stated to have been painter to the Prince of Wales. No.139 is a good example of his style, in which rather clumsy reminiscences of Rubens and Van Dyck are combined in an oddly neo-Titianesque spirit. In scale and feeling such pieces, reflecting the influence of Charles I's favour-ite painters, would have influenced Lely in his early years in England.

CORNELIUS JOHNSON (1593–1661) and GERARD HOUCKGEEST (*c.*1600–1661)

140. Henrietta Maria
Oil on panel: 19½ × 17 in.
Geoffrey Coldham, Esq.
No.140 illustrates, on a small scale, two practices current at the period: the copying on a reduced scale, and in different contexts, of successful portrait-types, and the use of fanciful perspectives, painted by specialists, as backgrounds. The panel was in Charles I's collection (the CR brand is on the back) and was described by Van der Doort (p.158). The portrait by Johnson was based on the image of the Queen in Van Dyck's double-portrait, now in Kremsier, but 'the Clothes are not as yet finished' and are clearly by a different hand. The perspective

134

135

137

139

136

138

is by Houckgeest. The King owned a number of
perspectives by him and Steenwyck and, in
addition, little perspectives by the latter in which
portraits of the King and Queen were painted by
Johnson and Belcamp (now in Dresden). Huge perspectives by Steenwyck appear behind the King in
portraits in Copenhagen and Turin; and one large
perspective setting was produced for Van Dyck to
put the King and Queen against: 'but Sir Anthony
van Dyck had no kind thereunto' (Van der Doort,
p.180; O. Millar in *Burl. Mag.*, vol. CIV (1962),
p.30).

The City and the Provinces

Only a partial impression of painting in the age of Charles I would be gained by looking merely at the painters employed in court circles. A number of less fortunate or accomplished painters were at work in the provinces, not unlike the Vicar of Wakefield's 'limner, who travelled the country, and took likenesses for fifteen shillings a head'. Many of them are anonymous. Men such as Souch are known only from work in a certain area. The better-known painters of this type, such as Jackson or Bower, were probably based in the capital and made periodical visits into the country in the service of groups of patrons. Such painters stood for a native tradition in painting and would have sympathised with the Company of Painter-Stainers in asserting claims to exercise control over all form of painting in London and in protesting against the success of the foreigners who had been attracted by asylum from religious persecution and by the patronage of the court. In 1627 a list of painters against whom the Company wished to proceed included the names of Gentileschi, Mytens, Priwitzer, Van der Doort and Steenwyck; and we find native-born painters such as Walker and Jackson prepared to support the Company. William Dobson was chosen by the Company, a few weeks before his death, to stand for nomination as Steward.

The painters who practised in the provinces and the City worked in an old-fashioned, linear, and often decorative style which carried the manner of Marcus Gheeraedts or Peake down to the end of our period with only passing recognition of Mytens or Van Dyck—in the fall of a curtain round a column or a gesture with a hand—and no grasp of their technique or understanding of the fundamentals of their styles. But their very provincialism enabled them to produce images which are of value to the social historian or the student of dress; and they composed scenes of everyday life and death which are made doubly moving by their lack of the technical accomplishment of a Van Dyck whose more sophisticated use of allusion and symbol made him incapable of recording such scenes with a gravity and realism to which one only finds parallels, in subject-matter and in spirit, in the funeral monuments of the age.

ROBERT PEAKE (*fl.*1587–1635)

141. Lady Margaret Russell (d.1676) and John Russell (1620–81)

Oil on canvas: $44\frac{1}{2} \times 34$ in. Inscribed with the ages (5 and 3) of the sitters and the date 1623, and, slightly later, the identities of the sitters.
His Grace the Duke of Bedford: Woburn Abbey Collections; repr. on p.90

Peake had been one of the most prolific and successful painters at the early Jacobean court. His *œuvre* has been reconstructed convincingly on the basis of a distinctive script used in inscriptions on his portraits. This script can be found on portraits as late as 1635 (a pair at Berkeley Castle). In 1607 he had been appointed Serjeant Painter jointly with John de Critz and had worked for Prince Henry and Prince Charles; but by *c.*1620 he had apparently been outclassed at court by the painters recently arrived from the Low Countries and his later portraits are in an almost archaic provincial tradition which links late Elizabethan painting with provincial painters working in the 1640s and in which the influence of Van Dyck, and even of Mytens and Johnson, is almost indiscernible (R. Strong, *The English Icon* (1969), pp.225–54).

Lady Margaret Russell, third daughter of the 4th Earl of Bedford, who had been painted by Peake as a

141

142

boy, married first (1632) the 2nd Earl of Carlisle and secondly (1667) the 2nd Earl of Manchester. Her brother John, the third son of the Earl, later commanded a regiment of foot in the royalist army (see No.165) and at the Restoration was appointed Colonel of the King's Regiment of Guards.

Attributed to JOHN (?) PARKER (*fl*.1632–7)

142. Eleanor Evelyn (1598–1635)

Oil on canvas: 44 × 33 in.
The Trustees of the will of J. H. C. Evelyn deceased, Christ Church, Oxford

The attribution is made on the basis of a portrait of a lady, signed and dated 1627 by Parker, which was on the art-market in London in 1953; with it can also perhaps be associated portraits at Ingatestone Hall of the 3rd Lord Petre (1635) and his son (1632) and, less convincingly, portraits of Richard (1635) and Elizabeth Evelyn (1634). William Sanderson, in his *Graphice* (1658), lists (p.20) a 'Mr. Parker' among amateur painters: 'worthy gentlemen, ingenious in their private delight'.

The pattern used for Mrs Evelyn is almost certainly derived from one of Van Dyck's earliest portraits of the Queen, the three-quarter-length, dated 1632, at Longford Castle; it was engraved by Pieter de Jode. Parker's portrait is an early instance, therefore, of the influence in England of Van Dyck's repertory of patterns.

Daughter of John Stansfield, she married Richard Evelyn in 1614. Their fourth child was John Evelyn, the diarist, who described his mother as 'of proper

personage, well timber'd, of a browne complexion; her eyes and haire of a lovely black; of constitution more inclyn'd to a religious Melancholy, or pious sadnesse'. Evelyn's brother George left the portrait, with others of his father and sister, to him in 1699.

143

GILBERT JACKSON (*fl.*1622-40)

143. **John, Lord Belasyse (1614–89)**

Oil on canvas: 74 × 51 in. Signed and dated: . . *Jack = /pinxit 1636*; repr. on p.90
The Duke of Hamilton and Brandon

Jackson's portraits, of which signed and dated examples are recorded between 1622 and 1640, show that he was in the habit of working in different parts of the country and had patrons in scholarly circles and among the country gentry. In December 1640 Jackson was sworn to the orders and ordinances of the Painter-Stainers, in order to be associated with their efforts to curb the activities of the 'Strangers'.

No.143 is a good example of the gay, two-dimensional, pattern and the lack of understanding of space and perspective which set such painters as Jackson apart from their rivals at court; but it is interesting to note how valuable such portraits are as illustrations of costume and furnishings.

Lord Belasyse was an active royalist in the Civil War. The identity of No.143 is, however, not fully established.

EDWARD BOWER (*d.*1666/7)

144. **Portrait of a Man**

Oil on canvas: 92 × 60 in. Signed: *Bower fecit* and inscribed with the date (1638) and the sitter's age (24); repr. on p.91
Lt Col G. W. Luttrell

Bower was almost certainly based in London. From 1629 he appears in the records of the Painter-Stainers Company, of which he became Master in 1661. On his earliest portraits (e.g., of 1637 and 1638) he described himself as 'Att Temple Barr', but he may have had patrons in the West Country. No.144 is the gayest and most dramatic of all Bower's surviving portraits; the pattern is perhaps closer in origin to Mytens than to Van Dyck and represents a distinctively English type of early baroque portrait. The twisted column had been used, in a rather modest manner, by Mytens in one of his official portraits of Charles I, and was used again by William Dobson. The most obvious source for it would have been in Raphael's Cartoon of *The Healing of the Lame Man*.

ARTIST UNKNOWN

145. **Margaret, Lady Verney (1594–1641)**

Oil on canvas: 29 × 24 in.
E. R. Verney, Esq.

Painted *c*.1635–40, and a charming example of the English provincial portrait. There is perhaps a suggestion of Van Dyckian elegance in the hands, but the mood and quality are still in the Gheeraedts tradition.

Daughter of Sir Thomas Denton, she married in 1612 Sir Edmund Verney, who fell as the King's Standard-Bearer at Edgehill. She was a devoted wife and mother to her twelve children. The allusions (the miniature in its 'picture-box' over her heart, the roses, the melancholy pose and the burns (?) on her left arm) have not been satisfactorily explained.

ARTIST UNKNOWN

146. **John Potkyn, Thomas Carleton and John Taylor**

Oil on canvas: 45 × 62¾ in. Dated 1631 and embellished with the arms of the three sitters.
The Worshipful Company of Painter-Stainers

The group was painted presumably soon after the election in October 1631 of Potkyn as Master, and of Carleton and Taylor as respectively Upper Warden and Renter Warden, of the Company. The picture was probably set up in the following autumn and would probably have been presented by the sitters to the Company. No.146 is a good and rare example of a civic group-portrait of the period (W. A. D. Englefield, *The History of the Painter-Stainers Company of London* (1950), pp. 17–20; J. Cornforth in *Country Life*, vol. CXLIX (1971), pp.978–8).

Attributed to DAVID DES GRANGES (1611 or 1613–1675(?))

147. **The Saltonstall Family**

Oil on canvas: 78 × 107 in. Sir Richard Salton-stall (d.1650) of Chipping Warden is seen approaching the bedside of his wife, Elizabeth, who has just been delivered of a child who is held in swaddling clothes by her bed. The children who accompany their father are prob-ably Richard (d.1688) and Anne; the baby may be the second son, Philip.
The Hon. Alan Clark

The traditional attribution to Des Granges is only called in question because the composition is of a scale and quality superior to anything else known from his brush; it is perhaps the most distinguished and charming work of its kind painted in England in the Stuart period.

JOHN SOUCH (*fl.*1616–1636)

148. **Sir Thomas Aston (1600–45) at the Death-Bed of his Wife**

Oil on canvas: 79¼ × 83¾ in. Signed: *Jo: Souch/ Cestrens/Fecit*; repr. on p.94
The inscriptions in Latin explain the events which are recorded. At the top are the arms of Sir Thomas and his wife Magdalene, daughter of Sir John Poultney, with inscriptions: *Arescit Corona mea* and *Virescit post funere virtus*. Lady

Aston had died in childbirth on 2 June 1635. In the picture she is seen on her death-bed and, again, seated in black at the foot of the bed. The cradle beside her is draped in black and under a skull, held on it by Sir Thomas, is the inscription: *Qui Spem carne seminat Metet ossa*. By his father, who was a royalist in the Civil War, stands his son Thomas, the only surviving child of the marriage, who died in fact two years later, in 1637. By him is an inscription: *fratris remulus, matris gloria, Solamen patris Ætat Suæ 3es Anni & 9em Menses*.

The picture is dated in the inscription above on the left: *Circumdederunt me dolores mortis/ Anno/Doloris et ætatis/35io/Septem: 30/16[3]5/ [Et ?] Ambu[larem] per valles umbrae/mortis non pertinescam/ . . . Consolabor.*

The little boy holds a cross- or fore-staff, a navigational or surveying instrument, perhaps to be linked with the celestial globe. The table-cloth is a painted cotton cloth from Masula-patan. On it rests an unstrung lute (C. H. Collins Baker in the *Connoisseur*, vol. LXXX (1928), pp.131–3).
The City of Manchester Art Galleries

Souch was a Chester painter whose *œuvre* consists of a very small group of portraits of patrons living in that part of the world, e.g. the *Roger Puleston* in the Tate Gallery. It is not surprising that he should have been recorded in 1616–17 as apprenticed to a herald painter in Chester.

149

148

ARTIST UNKNOWN

149. **The Salusbury Family**
Oil on canvas: 76 × 99 in.
Edmund Brudenell, Esq.

Probably painted *c*.1640. Sir Thomas Salusbury (d.1643), 2nd Baronet of Llewenny, was Colonel of a regiment of foot raised for the King in the Civil War in the Counties of Denbigh and Flint. In No.149 there may be allusions to the war but it is more likely to be a hunting piece. Sir Thomas married before August 1632 Hester, widow of Sir Peter Lemaire, daughter of Sir Edward Tyrell. The boy with two hounds is probably Thomas (1634–58), later the 3rd Baronet; the girl would be Hester (d.1710), who married Sir Robert Cotton; the baby is probably John (d.1684), the 4th and last Baronet.

The group cannot be attributed with confidence to any known painter and is perhaps an exceptionally ambitious work by one of the provincial painters who had patrons in the Welsh Marches.

NICHOLAS LANIER (1588–1666)

150. **Portrait of the Artist**
Oil on canvas: 26 × 23 in. Under a skull by the artist's right arm, and near the brush which is poised above his palette, is a skull lying on a sheet of music to the words: 'Thus. thus. at last wee must reduced/be to naked boanes and dust'. Signed: *made, and/paynted by/Nich: Lanier.* Lanier himself presented the portrait to the Music School.
The Faculty of Music, University of Oxford

Probably painted *c*.1640, No.150 makes an interesting comparison with the portrait of Lanier by Van Dyck (No.74). The *Self-portrait*, far more provincial in quality, shows Lanier in his capacity as a painter and not as an emissary of the King (Mrs. R. L. Poole, *Catalogue of Portraits . . .*, vol. I (1912), p.154).

The Civil War

'In growing and enlarging times, Arts are commonly drowned in Action'. The effect of the Civil Wars was to destroy the brittle fabric of the civilisation of the Caroline court. Its collapse can be dated from the departure of the royal family from Whitehall on 10 January 1642, a month (incidentally) after the death of Van Dyck in his house at Blackfriars. Enlightened royal patronage was at an end and the valuable cultural links with the Continent were almost entirely severed. It was *le turbolenze* which prevented the Queen from sending her portraits by Van Dyck out to Rome for Bernini to use as material for another marble bust; but it is important to note that in the last years of his life the King was still discussing with John Webb plans for a vast baroque palace at Whitehall. Those artists were most fortunate who found patrons among members of the court circle who had not followed the King: the artists and craftsmen who worked for the Earl of Pembroke, under the eyes of Jones and Webb, at Wilton and carried on the architectural and decorative principles first demonstrated in happier times; or Peter Lely who found a generous patron in the Earl of Northumberland. The court at Oxford must, by contrast, have been a much less settled and congenial place in which to work. During the Civil Wars and Interregnum there was no lack of demand from patrons for 'their own dull counterfeits', in Lovelace's contemptuous phrase, and in Samuel Cooper this period produced perhaps the greatest English portrait-painter of the age; but in 'this un-understanding land' there was now little demand for other subjects from a painter: for the images which Jordaens, Van Dyck, Guido Reni or Gentileschi would have produced. Militant puritanism, indeed, always hostile to the arts of a court so tainted with Catholicism and now let loose in the war like a personification by Rubens, was responsible for an enormous amount of wanton loot and for waves of savage and organised iconoclasm (see No.177) which recall the worst excesses of the Reformation. Sir Robert Harley's committee for the destruction of idolatrous and superstitious monuments did most damage to the royal chapels; but it was principally economic need and financial duress, rather than such fanatisism, which caused the sale of almost all the great Whitehall collections, which brings to an end on a note of high tragedy and incalculable loss the story of the arts under Charles I.

155

119

WILLIAM DOBSON (1611–46)

151. Portrait of the Artist with Sir Charles Cotterell (1612(?)–1702) and an Elderly Man
Oil on canvas: $38\frac{1}{2} \times 49\frac{1}{2}$ in., repr. on p.100
The Duke of Northumberland

Dobson is the most interesting and accomplished native-born English painter 'in large' in the seventeenth century, described by a contemporary as 'the most excellent painter that England hath yet bred'. He seems to have moved in artistic circles at court before the Civil War and to have benefited from seeing the great Caroline collections: experiences that account for the Caravaggesque and Venetian, as well as the Van Dyckian, elements in his style. Nothing of his work is known, however, before he is found established at the unsettled wartime court at Oxford in 1642, painting the King, his family and principal supporters. He left Oxford in 1646, probably soon after the King had departed, with most of Dobson's patrons, in April. He died, obviously in great poverty, in his house in St. Martin's Lane. His career, for all its sad end, is significant for the influence on a young English artist of the cultural achievements and ideals of the Caroline court.

In No.151 Dobson is seen embracing his friend Cotterell (see No.153) and apparently turning away, or being protected, from a gentleman who is usually (but probably wrongly) identified with Sir Balthasar Gerbier who played a long and frequently discreditable role in diplomacy and in the service of, or otherwise in association with, the collectors and artists of the Jacobean and Caroline age. He leans on a partly concealed bust (perhaps of Apollo) and holds a drawing of Venus and Cupid (?) (for Dobson, see particularly O. Millar, Tate Gallery exhibition (1951); W. Vaughan, *Endymion Porter & William Dobson*, Tate Gallery (1970)).

152. Portrait of an Unknown Officer with a Page
Oil on canvas: $56 \times 45\frac{1}{2}$ in. Inscribed and dated: *An°. Dm̄i, 1642./Ætis Suæ, 50*
The Lord Sackville

The earliest dated portrait by Dobson, probably representing an officer in the King's service. The paint is very richly applied; the stormy background and the motive of the attendant page with the gauntlet are fundamentally Venetian, but had been used by Van Dyck; the martial presentation is slightly reminiscent of Miereveld or Ravesteyn; but the bluff English mood, frontal position of the sitter

and heavy column reveal in embryo the distinctively English form of baroque portrait which Dobson was developing and which reaches its climax in No.155.

153. Sir Charles Cotterell
Oil on canvas (octagonal): $21\frac{1}{4} \times 17\frac{3}{4}$ in. Inscribed with the names of artist and sitter.
Private Collection

Painted at Oxford c.1643. The sitter, Master of Ceremonies to Charles I and II, was clearly a friend of the painter, and may have helped to introduce him into scholarly circles at Oxford.

154. The Civil Wars of France
Oil on canvas: $49 \times 57\frac{1}{2}$ in.; repr. on p.100
Private Collection

Painted at Oxford, presumably under the supervision of Sir Charles Cotterell, who was engaged with Sir Thomas Aylesbury on a translation of Davila's *Istoria delle guerre civili di Francia* (1630). The theme had obvious significance at the time Dobson was painting. In a desolate landscape the two last Valois kings of France, Charles IX and Henry III, stand near the Huguenot and Catholic hounds who struggle over the prostrate figure of France. She is rescued by Henry IV. St. Louis in the background views the scene with despair. In the figures in feigned relief in the surrounding framework the horrors of civil strife are contrasted with the blessings of peace. The framework is reminiscent of decorative work by Francis Cleyn, most of it for borders of tapestries woven at Mortlake, and confirms the very early tradition that Dobson had studied with Cleyn.

155. Charles II when Prince of Wales
Oil on canvas: $59\frac{1}{2} \times 50\frac{1}{2}$ in.; repr. on p.97
The Scottish National Portrait Gallery

Probably painted in 1643 and traditionally stated to have been commissioned to commemorate the battle of Edgehill at which the King's two eldest sons were present with their tutor. The Prince holds a commander's baton and wears the badge of the Garter over his breastplate. The page is traditionally identified with Francis Wyndham, one of the Prince's attendants.

No.155 is the most sumptuous example of the full-blown baroque style towards which Dobson was moving in his portrait of 1642. It is still very rich in texture and, by cutting off the design at a very unorthodox point below his knees, the sitter is thrust forward at the spectator in a thoroughly un-Van Dyckian way. The colours and weapons heaped over

153

151

158

154

152

156

157

a head of Medusa and the distant battle have a dramatic immediacy no less foreign to Van Dyck.

156. **Prince Rupert with Colonel William Murray (d.1652(?)) and Colonel John Russell**

Oil on canvas: $59\frac{1}{4} \times 78\frac{1}{4}$ in.
Private Collection

Probably painted *c*.1644 and traditionally stated to record the moment when Murray and the Prince persuaded Russell (see No.165) to renew the commission which he had given up in disgust. With No.151, it is one of the earliest group-portraits painted in England which has the air of a conversation piece: at the outset, that is to say, of the tradition which was to be developed by Highmore and Hogarth in the eighteenth century. The force of the scene is strengthened by the almost complete absence of anything approaching Van Dyck's elegance.

157. **Sir William Compton (1625–63)**

Oil on canvas: 89×58 in. Inscribed later: *Sir WILL^M COMPTON K^N*.
The Marquess of Northampton

Probably painted *c*.1644; Dobson's paint is becoming rougher and drier than it was in No.152 or 155. Perhaps as a result of his early training with Cleyn, and of his association with learned circles in Oxford, Dobson frequently made allusion, through busts or reliefs of classical subjects, to the nature or occupation of his sitters. The battle in the relief on the base of the column would be appropriate for any of the gallant Compton brothers who were devoted royalists. Sir William was a younger brother of the 3rd Earl of Northampton. The portrait is one of only two known full-lengths by Dobson and is one of his most compelling presentations of a fighting royalist officer.

158. **Inigo Jones (1573–1652)**

Oil on canvas (circular): $23\frac{1}{4}$ in., but probably cut down from *c*.30×25 in. to enable it to fit into Lord Burlington's scheme of decoration in the Red Velvet Room at Chiswick.
The Department of the Environment, Chiswick House

Probably painted *c*.1644, and a moving commentary on the old architect's appearance during these unhappy years. It would certainly have been painted before his capture at the fall of Basing House on 14 October 1645.

159. Prince Rupert

Oil on canvas: $28\frac{1}{2} \times 23\frac{1}{2}$ in.

Private Collection

Probably left unfinished when Rupert left Oxford early in 1646 after his quarrel with his uncle. A number of portraits seem to have been left unfinished by Dobson owing to the departure of the King on 27 April 1646. The portrait, with its thinned texture and lack of substance, is as vivid a commentary on the unhappy career of the Prince at this time as on the impoverishment of Dobson's technique.

ROBERT WALKER (d.1658)

160. Portrait of the Artist

Oil on canvas: 29×24 in. Signed: *R. Walker: pict et pinx. . .* : the area on which the signature occurs is damaged

The Visitors of the Ashmolean Museum, Oxford

Walker was the painter principally employed by the parliamentarians: Cromwell, Ireton, Fairfax, Lambert and Colonel Hutchinson were among his more prominent sitters. He almost slavishly exploited Van Dyck's patterns for such sitters. The design of the *Self-portrait* reflects perhaps a knowledge of Van Dyck's (No.92). Mercury is introduced as the patron of the arts: the role he plays, personified by the Duke of Buckingham, in Honthorst's *Apollo and Diana* (No.78).

161. John Evelyn (1620–1706)

Oil on canvas: $34\frac{1}{2} \times 25\frac{1}{4}$ in. Inscribed with a quotation from Seneca's *Epistle XXX* and with the dictum, in Greek, that 'Repentance is the beginning of Wisdom'.

The Trustees of the Will of J. H. C. Evelyn deceased, Christ Church, Oxford

On 1 July 1648 Evelyn 'sate for my *Picture* (the same wherein is a *Deaths head*) to Mr. *Walker* that excellent Painter'. With its standard presentation of Melancholy and its funereal reminder of mortality, it was designed by Evelyn to accompany a treatise on marriage which he had prepared for his young wife Mary Browne, whom he had married in Paris in 1647. He had intended originally that the piece should have been painted, as a miniature, by Peter Oliver, Hoskins or Johnson (W. G. Hiscock, *John Evelyn and his Family Circle* (1955), pp. 20–21).

162. The Children of the 5th Earl of Dorset

Oil on canvas: 54×90 in. On the back is an early inscription, copied presumably from the back of the original canvas, giving Walker as the painter.

The Lord Sackville

Probably painted in the early years of the Commonwealth, the children are Charles, Lord Buckhurst (b.1638), the future 6th Earl of Dorset, with Edward (b.1641) and Mary (b.1646) Sackville. The Arcadian convention shows, as do some of Lely's portraits of this date, the influence of Van Dyck; the pastiche of a Titianesque landscape is a reminder that Walker had copied Titians in Charles I's collection.

CORNELIUS DE NEVE (fl.1627–1664)

163. Portrait of the Artist

Oil on canvas: $26\frac{1}{2} \times 22\frac{1}{2}$ in. Inscribed later with the sitter's name.

The Visitors of the Ashmolean Museum, Oxford

Probably painted c.1645. De Neve was apparently at work in England over a long period; his portraits are normally cast in the Anglo-Netherlandish mould, but are dry and rather provincial in texture (Mrs. R. L. Poole, *Catalogue of Portraits . . .*, vol. I (1912), p.178).

JOAN CARLILE (1606(?)–1679)

164. A Stag Hunt

Oil on canvas: $24 \times 29\frac{1}{8}$ in., repr. on p.104

Sir Gyles Isham, Bt.

Joan Carlile was an amateur painter of some distinction and with influential patrons before the Civil War, during the Interregnum and after the Restoration. The daughter of William Palmer, an official in the royal parks, she married in 1626 Lodowick Carlile, Gentleman of the Bows to Charles I and one of the keepers at Richmond Park. He was a minor poet and dramatist and an enthusiastic huntsman who described himself as one who 'hunts and hawks, and feeds his Deer, Not some, but most fair days throughout the yeer'. In No.164, painted in 1649 or 1650, the Carliles are seen, presumably in Richmond Park, with their children James and Penelope, their friend Sir Justinian Isham and others (unidentified).

Mrs Carlile may have known Van Dyck. Certainly his influence is discernible in her little single full-length portraits. No.164 is also one of the most charming premonitions, painted in England in the Stuart period, of the conversation-piece in a landscape: the genre to be developed in the eighteenth century by Devis, Hogarth and Zoffany (M. Toynbee and Sir G. Isham in *Burl. Mag.*, vol. XCVI (1954), pp.275–7; *The Correspondence of Bishop Brian Duppa and Sir Justinian Isham*, ed. Sir G. Isham (1955), pp.33–34).

165

164

167

168

JOHN HAYLS (d.1680)

165. Colonel John Russell

Oil on canvas: 44½ × 34½ in.

The Trustees of the Warwick Castle Resettlement

Formerly identified (and so inscribed) as
Robert, 2nd Lord Brooke (1608–43), but clearly of a
younger sitter and a slightly later date (c.1645). The
sitter can be safely identified with Lord Brooke's
brother-in-law, Colonel Russell (see No.156), of
whom there is a portrait of this period by Hayls at
Woburn. Hayls's career at this period is very obscure, but his *œuvre* can be partly reconstructed
around a group of portraits of the Russells and
Grevilles. No.165, a good example of his style during
the Civil War, shows him painting in a rather
coarsened Van Dyckian style and in a mood which
seems English and thus close to Dobson.

GERARD SOEST (d.1681)

166. Constantine(?) Lyttelton (1632–63)

Oil on canvas: 28⅛ × 23¼ in. Signed: *Soest.*
Inscribed later with the sitter's name and
age (18).

The Viscount Cobham

One of a set of portraits, of which some are
dated 1651 and which are stated to be of the
sons of Sir Thomas Lyttelton; some of the
identifications present difficulties. No.166 was early
inscribed as being of Ferdinando, the eleventh son.
Soest had probably arrived in London from Holland
before the execution of Charles I. Some of his
earliest portraits have a Dobsonesque richness of
texture. No.166 is a good example of the highly
personal, sombre mood and distinguished technique
which, even at this early date, set Soest apart from
all his contemporaries.

THEODORE RUSSELL (1614–89)

167. Portrait of a Man

Oil on canvas: 29 × 24 in. Signed and dated:
T. Russel: 1644 (initials in monogram)

The Hon David Lytton-Cobbold

The painter was a nephew of Cornelius

Johnson, whose influence is clearly discernible in
No.167 and in the four (unsigned) companion female
portraits with which it hangs at Knebworth. Documented works by Russell are extremely rare; he is
often associated, not entirely convincingly, with
small copies on panel of portraits by Van Dyck.

ARTIST UNKNOWN

168. John Tradescant the Younger (1608–62)

Oil on canvas: 42 × 34 in. Inscribed later with
the sitter's name, 'in his Garden'

The Visitors of the Ashmolean Museum, Oxford

The sitter succeeded his father as Gardener to
Henrietta Maria. As a collector he was perhaps the
first man in England to put forward the idea of a
museum. His heterogeneous collections, part of
which he had inherited from his father, were kept at
Lambeth and were described in his *Musaeum Trade-
scantianum* (1656). He rashly settled his 'Closet of
Rarities' on his friend Elias Ashmole.

No.168, one of the most moving portraits of the
period, is in a set of portraits which passed into
Ashmole's possession and which, with a related
portrait in the National Portrait Gallery, continue to
defy attribution; one of the set, a portrait of Mrs
Tradescant and her son, is dated 1645. In mood the
portraits have something in common with Soest; in
quality they are far more distinguished than anything known by John de Critz the Younger or his
son Emmanuel with whom the set is sometimes
asscoiated; but one of the portraits in the set is of
Oliver de Critz, of whom very little is known but
who is described on the canvas as 'A famous Painter'
(Mrs R. L. Poole, *Catalogue of Portraits . . .*, vol. I
(1912), pp.175–6).

169. Abraham Stanyan

Oil on canvas: 42¼ × 33¼ in. Inscribed with the
date (1644) and the sitter's age (33).

Private Collection

The halberd and the plumed hat probably
indicate that the sitter was a member of the Band of
Gentlemen Pensioners. The portrait is exhibited to
represent the kind of problem that is presented in
this period. The portrait, both in type and in texture,
is very near to Dobson; but it is a little smoother
and is just conceivably an early work by Soest.

SIR PETER LELY (1618–80)

170. **An Idyll**

Oil on canvas: 48¾ × 92¼ in.

The Courtauld Institute of Art (Lee Collection)

Lely is not recorded certainly in London before 1647 and his earliest works in England included 'Landtschapes, with *small Figures*, and *Historical Compositions*'. His friend Richard Lovelace regretted in his panegyric, *Peinture*, addressed to Lely, that they had met with such little success in England. No.170 is one of the finest of such compositions. The scale, and the relation of the figures to the landscape, are Netherlandish: reminiscent of Poelenburgh (No.138) or Wouters(No.139) among painters who had worked earlier in England and with the same echoes of Titian and Van Dyck that are to be discerned in Wouters's compositions.

The subject has not been satisfactorily explained, but although it is almost certainly wrong to describe it as 'Lely and his Family' (a title it has borne since at least 1763), the figures, who occur in other subject-pieces by Lely, were clearly members of his circle in the late 1640's (P. Murray, *The Lee Collection* (1958), No. 38).

171. **Charles I with James, Duke of York**

Oil on canvas: 49¾ × 57¾ in.

The Duke of Northumberland

Nos.171 and 172, painted by Lely for the Earl of Northumberland (No.102) are the first important and securely dated works in his career in England, where the Earl was probably his first influential patron. The younger royal children were in Northumberland's care at Syon and were allowed, during 1647, to visit their father who was then at Hampton Court, where he presumably gave a sitting to Lely. In 1648 the painter was paid £20 by the Earl 'for the King and the Duke of Yorkes pickture in one piece'. It inspired a eulogy from Lovelace: 'on that excellent Picture of his Majesty, and the Duke of Yorke, drawne . . . at Hampton Court'. Although the figures are rather wooden, the handling and use of colour are finer than those of any other painter then working in England.

172. **The Three Children of Charles I**

Oil on canvas: 78½ × 91¾ in. Inscribed with the titles and ages of the children. They are James, Duke of York (later James II, see No.105), Princess Elizabeth (see No.105) and Henry, Duke of Gloucester (1639–1660); repr. on p.108

The National Trust and H.M. Treasury (Egremont Collection, Petworth)

Painted for the Earl of Northumberland in 1647. It was noted in the Earl's collection at Suffolk

171

House in 1652. Although to some extent a re-interpretation of Van Dyck's portrait-groups of the royal children, No.172 is infused with a rich Dutch baroque spirit, in the quality of paint, in details such as the sculptured fountain and in the dramatic landscape which is reminiscent of Dutch Italianate landscape painting.

173. **Lady Elizabeth Percy, Countess of Essex (1636–1718)**
Oil on canvas: 46½ × 39 in., repr. on p.108
The National Trust (Egremont Collection, Petworth)
The sitter was daughter of the Earl of Northumberland; in 1653 she married Arthur Capel, later 1st Earl of Essex. No.173 is among the portraits of the Earl's family painted by Lely *c.*1650. It shows

the extent of Van Dyck's influence upon him at this early period. The design is a clumsy derivation from Van Dyck's portrait of Lady Elizabeth's cousin, Dorothy, Countess of Sunderland, which had been painted for Northumberland twenty years earlier.

174. **Henry Marten (1602–80)**
Oil on canvas: 29 × 24 in. Inscribed later: *now The Rt. Hon. Hugh Fraser* repr. on p.108
Probably painted *c.*1647–50, at a time when Lely's sitters are not placed with complete conviction on the canvas. The sitter was a convinced republican and a regicide, but as, in Aubrey's words, 'a lover of pretty girles', he offended his associates. At the Restoration he was imprisoned for life. The inscription presumably refers to his determination to extirpate the monarchy.

172

173

174

175

EDWARD BOWER (d.1666/7)

175. Charles I at his Trial
    Oil on canvas: $51\frac{5}{8} \times 37\frac{7}{8}$ in. Signed and dated:
    Edw. Bower./att Temple Barr./fecit 1648.
    Formerly in the collection of the Earls of
    Winchilsea and Nottingham; last sold at
    Christie's, 6 April 1951 (135), when it was
    purchased by H.M. Queen Elizabeth, The
    Queen Mother.
    *Her Majesty Queen Elizabeth, The Queen
    Mother*
    One of four known signed and dated variants
of a portrait presumably painted by Bower on the
basis of drawings made on the spot in Westminster
Hall, during the King's trial before the High Court
of Justice on 20, 22, 23 and 27 January 1649. Although the original commission may have been given
by one of the King's opponents, the pattern became
popular with royalists. Many later copies and
derivations are known. In style the pattern is very
old-fashioned: painted without any thought of Van
Dyck and in the old provincial and City tradition
(Millar, *Tudor, Stuart*, No.208; to which should be
added a signed and dated version in the collection of
Mr J. H. Thursby).

GODDARD DUNNING (c.1614–1678)

176. Charles I
    Oil on canvas: $31\frac{3}{4} \times 26\frac{3}{4}$ in. Signed and dated:
    Dunning fecit/1649
    Miss Joan Wadge
    The King is seen wearing the clothes he wore
at his execution; it is perhaps the earliest representation of the King at that moment, possibly
based on notes made on the spot and painted by an
artist who appears to have specialised in pictures of
the King at the end of his life: as late as 1677 he
made a little copy of a version of No.175. The type
was developed as one of the standard images of the
Martyr King.

THOMAS JOHNSON (fl.1634–85)

177. Iconoclasts in Canterbury Cathedral
    Oil on canvas: 24×41 in. Signed and dated:
    *Thos. Johnson fecit. Canterbury Quire as in
    1657/Y^e prospecte from y^e Clock House*
    A. D. R. Caroe, Esq., under Trust
    The view is taken from the top of Prior Chil-
lenden's pulpitum, under the Angel Tower or Clock
House. A parliamentary committee is apparently
directing the destruction of stained glass and carved
decoration (W. D. Caroe in *Archaeologia*, vol. LXII
(1911), pp.353–66). Johnson was a loyal member of
the Painter-Stainers Company and is significant as a
topographical painter and draughtsman, influenced
by Hollar, and apparently especially active in
Canterbury.

The Miniature

Charles I was probably the first collector to form, in the modern sense, a collection of miniatures. In his 'new erected' Cabinet Room at Whitehall, in which he had put together his smallest, most highly prized and most exotic possessions, were cupboards in which were laid out nearly eighty 'lim'd peeces': set in simple turned 'boxes' of ivory, amber, ebony, jet and boxwood; in 'a round golden blew and white enamuled ring', or 'a goulden square enamoled wrought Case', specially made to hold a miniature of the Queen.

The surpassing excellence of miniature painting in England in the lifetime of Charles I is owing partly to the delight which patrons and connoisseurs took in the ingenious and the 'curious'—in fine workmanship on an intricate scale—and partly to the intimate nature of the miniature itself as a form of portraiture. It was at once more precious and more portable than a portrait 'in large'. Miniatures were sent overseas in jewelled settings, as presents to foreign rulers; even Cromwell's portrait in limning was presented by the Council of State as reward for services to the state or as tokens of friendship. More significant: miniatures were painted and displayed as special tokens of affection, tied, for example, by a black ribbon over the heart of a mourning widow (No.101). They would convey a specially personal message. It is significant that Evelyn had intended at first that the piece of moralising for his wife's ear, actually painted 'in large' by Walker, should have been entrusted to a miniaturist. It was in the intimacy of the miniature that Norgate (No.208) or Sir Kenelm Digby could express their private griefs.

There is a very close connection in this period between painting in miniature and on the scale of life. Patrons found it useful to commission copies in miniature, from big portraits, for distribution to friends: Strafford employed Hoskins in this way over his own portrait by Van Dyck; the copies by Peter Oliver of Van Dyck's portraits of the Digbys formed part of Sir Kenelm's monument to his wife and her virtues; Des Granges's copies of a standard portrait of the young Charles II (No.224) were distributed among his supporters; and Petitot's copies in enamel seem to have been specially prized. The copies made by Peter Oliver of Charles I's great Italian pictures would have compelled the miniaturist to absorb something of their influence. Conversely, one often finds a painter on a large scale making use of a miniature done *ad vivum*; in putting together a portrait of Ireton, Robert Walker makes use of Samuel Cooper's portrait (No.219), presumably because the sitter was dead.

Stylistically there are also affinities between the two scales. In Gheeraedts and Peake we see carried on in the age of Charles I something of the linear quality, delight in pattern, and sensitive personality of Nicholas Hilliard; his son Laurence still displays these qualities on the eve of the Civil War. The more confident manner of Isaac Oliver echoes the rich, brassy tone of the Jacobean full-length portrait, but his son Peter Oliver reveals something of the more sympathetic and naturalistic style of Mytens or Cornelius Johnson. This is also true of Hoskins, whose style was subsequently affected by Van Dyck, whom he copied, often on an unusually large scale. It was an influence that he could not easily digest; but it is the especial distinction of Samuel Cooper, Hoskins's nephew, that he absorbed all that he needed from the inspiration of Van Dyck and combined it with his own remarkable technical gifts, rare sympathy and psychological penetration. His portraits are unsurpassed as revelations of English character in those distracted times and it is an almost inadequate tribute 'that he was commonly stil'd the *Van-Dyck* in little'.

178   180   181

NICHOLAS HILLIARD (1547–1619)

178. Henry, Prince of Wales (1594–1612)
Watercolour on vellum, oval: $2\frac{3}{8} \times 2$ in. Inscribed: *Ano. Dñi. 1607 Ætatis suæ 14*. Presumably painted for James I. In the collection of Charles I: 'Done by the ould Hilliard . . .' (E. Auerbach, *Nicholas Hilliard* (1961), p.314, No.158).
Her Majesty The Queen
Hilliard was Limner to the King and received payments for royal portraits almost up to the time of his death; but his portraits of the new dynasty are among his least distinguished and original productions. It is not surprising that Prince Henry should have preferred the work of Hilliard's rival, Isaac Oliver. Hilliard's style seems, by contrast, to be in an English, even by now a provincial, tradition.

ISAAC OLIVER (c.1565–1617)

179. Henry, Prince of Wales
Watercolour on vellum: $5\frac{1}{8} \times 4$ in., repr. on p.98
Her Majesty The Queen
Probably painted *c.*1612. Described in Charles I's collection as 'the biggest lim'd Picture that was made by Prince Henry . . .' (Van der Doort, p.107).

Oliver had come over from Rouen with his father, a Huguenot refugee, in 1568. By 1604 he had become Queen Anne's Limner and he was also attached to the Household of Prince Henry. The magnificent confidence, quality and scale of this miniature is in contrast with the restraint of Hilliard's presentation. A number of smaller repetitions of it were commissioned and it was the source from which Mytens and Van Dyck worked up posthumous portraits for Charles I.

180. Charles I when Duke of York
Watercolour on vellum, oval: $2\frac{1}{8} \times 1\frac{5}{8}$ in.
Her Majesty The Queen
Probably painted just before the death of Henry, Prince of Wales, in 1612. In Charles I's collection: 'Don by the life by Isack: Oliver . . .' (Van der Doort, p.112).

181. Princess Elizabeth (1596–1662), later Queen of Bohemia
Watercolour on vellum, oval: $2 \times 1\frac{5}{8}$ in.
Signed with the monogram IO.
Her Majesty The Queen
Painted *c.*1610, before her marriage (in 1613), to the Elector Palatine. In the collection of Charles I: '. . . . your Ma^ts Sister when she was younger in her high time past fashioned haire dressing adorn'd at

her head wth some single Elengtine Roases wth Jewells and Pearls and a neck lace w^th.3. Jewells about her neck and her habbitt adorn'd all over wth Carnation and White Ribbons . . .' (Van der Doort, p.117).

182. Portrait of a Young Man as the Prodigal Son

Watercolour on vellum, oval: $2\frac{13}{16} \times 2\frac{1}{16}$ in.

The Duke of Portland

Painted *c*.1612; in the collection of Charles I: 'Done by Isack Oliver . . . a Certaine naked young mans picture to the wast holding both his hands Crosse over another upon his breast . . .' (Van der Doort, p.120; Goulding, No.34).

183. Queen Anne of Denmark (1574–1619)

Watercolour on vellum, oval: $2 \times 1\frac{5}{8}$ in. Signed with the monogram IO and inscribed: *Servo per regnare*.

Her Majesty The Queen

The most brilliant and evocative of the portraits of the Queen by 'her Ma^tes painter for the Art of Lymning', showing her in an elaborate masquing costume, reminiscent of Jones's designs for Jonson's *Masque of Queens* of 1609.

ARTIST UNKNOWN

184. Charles I when Duke of York

Watercolour on vellum, oval: $1\frac{7}{16} \times 1\frac{1}{16}$ in. A lock of the Prince's hair is enclosed in the back of the miniature.

Her Majesty The Queen

Painted in the style of Nicholas Hilliard, *c*.1611, the year in which the Prince received the Garter.

PETER OLIVER (*c*.1594–1647)

185. Charles I when Prince of Wales

Watercolour on vellum, oval: $2\frac{1}{8} \times 1\frac{3}{4}$ in. Signed with the monogram PO and dated 1621.

Her Majesty The Queen

186. Sir Robert Harley (1580–1656)

Watercolour on vellum, oval: $2\frac{3}{8} \times 11\frac{15}{16}$ in. Signed with the monogram PO and inscribed *ter & amplius*.

The Duke of Portland

Painted *c*.1620–25. The sitter, who wears the ribbon of the Bath, was a high-minded puritan and chairman of a committee, set up by Parliament in 1643, for the destruction of idolatrous or superstitious monuments. He was particularly active in dismantling the royal chapels and in reporting on 'superstitious pictures'.

Both miniatures are good examples of the developments made by Peter Oliver from the manner of his father: towards a more relaxed, more naturalistic, and more painterly presentation, qualities which reflect the influence of such painters as Daniel Mytens working on the scale of life.

187. Sir Kenelm Digby (1603–65) and his Family

Watercolour on vellum: $6\frac{1}{8} \times 9\frac{3}{4}$ in. Signed, dated and inscribed: *Invenit Eq Van Dyck / Imitatus est P.O. / 1635* and *Ponderibus librata suis*.

The Nationalmuseum, Stockholm

A copy from Van Dyck's life-size group, painted in 1632, of which versions are at Sherborne Castle and Welbeck; in the royal collection is a version of the father cut from another version of the group. For Lady Digby see No.107; the two sons are Kenelm (1625–48) and John (b.1627) Digby (T. H. Colding, *Aspects of Miniature Painting* (1953), pp.119, 204).

Sir Kenelm, 'a person very eminent and notorious throughout the whole course of his life', was active in the fields of diplomacy, letters, science and seafaring. He was a close friend of Van Dyck, bound to him by 'una vicendevole collegatione di genio, e di benevolenza'. Van Dyck made religious pictures for him; and Digby in Rome gave material to Bellori for his *Vita* of the painter. He was one of Van Dyck's first patrons in England in 1632.

188. Sir Kenelm Digby: Venetia, Lady Digby

Watercolour on vellum, each $3\frac{1}{2}$ in. in height. Set as a little diptych in a fine contemporary case. The portrait of Sir Kenelm is inscribed: *Vindica te tibi*. The companion is inscribed and dated: *The La: Ve Digby : A : D; 1632. Æt : 32 Simon Wingfield Digby, Esq.*

The portraits are copied from the same source as No.187.

189. Venetia, Lady Digby, on her Death bed

Watercolour on vellum: height $2\frac{5}{8}$ in. Inscribed and dated: *The La: Ve: Digby: / A.D. 1633 Æt. 32. M.4.D.12.* Set in a fine contemporary case.

183 184 185

186

187

Simon Wingfield Digby, Esq.

A copy in miniature of the portrait, commissioned by Sir Kenelm from Van Dyck, of which a good version is at Dulwich: 'the Master peece', in Sir Kenelm's words, 'of all the excellent ones that ever Sir Antony Vandike made, who drew her the second day after she was dead; and hath expressed with admirable art every little circumstance about her . . . and hath altered or added nothing about it, excepting only a rose . . . whose leaves being pulled from the stalke in the full beauty of it . . . is a fitt Embleme to express the state her bodie then was in'. The painting became Sir Kenelm's constant companion; he mourned his wife despairingly and added to his tributes to her the posthumous allegory by Van Dyck (No.107) (V. Gabrieli, *Sir Kenelm Digby* (Rome, 1957), pp. 246–9).

190. **After Correggio: Jupiter and Antiope**
Watercolour on vellum: $8\frac{1}{4} \times 5\frac{3}{8}$ in. Signed and dated: *Anº. Do. 1633, Anton: Coregium. Imitatus est. Petr. Olivarius.*
Her Majesty The Queen

One of the copies in miniature, painted for Charles I, after some of the principal Italian renaissance masterpieces in his collection. The source, which is now in the Louvre, was among the pictures acquired by Charles I with the Mantuan collection (Oppé, No.463). Payment for the little copies may have been included in the £200 paid to the artist by the King in 1635 for pictures made and to be made. They were kept in cupboards in the Cabinet Room at Whitehall, 'in double shutting Cases with Locks and keys and glasses over them' (Van der Doort, pp.102–5).

JOHN HOSKINS (c.1595–1665)

191. **Catherine Howard, Countess of Salisbury (d.1673)**
Watercolour on vellum, oval: $2\frac{1}{8} \times 1\frac{7}{8}$ in.
Signed with the monogram IH.
The Earl Beauchamp
Painted *c.*1618; a replica is in the possession of the Duke of Rutland. The miniature shows Hoskins working in a style which is close in mood to contemporary portraits by Gheeraedts or Jonson, before his style expanded, partly under the influence of Van Dyck and his own nephew Samuel Cooper. The sitter, a daughter of the Earl of Suffolk, married the 2nd Earl of Salisbury in 1608.

192. **Charles I**
Watercolour on vellum: $8\frac{1}{2} \times 6\frac{3}{32}$ in. Signed:
I H ft, under the King's crown, monogram and the date 1632.
The Earl Beauchamp
The largest and most important of Hoskins's portraits of the King, apparently painted from life.

193. **Henrietta Maria**
Watercolour on vellum: $8\frac{1}{2} \times 5\frac{3}{4}$ in. Inscribed with the Queen's cipher under a crown.
The Devonshire Collection, Chatsworth. Lent by the Trustees of the Chatsworth Settlement
Hoskins painted a number of miniatures of the Queen from life and also from Van Dyck's portraits of her. No.193 is based on one of the standard Van Dyckian types behind which Hoskins introduces a charming little landscape of London.

194. **James I**
Watercolour on vellum, oval: $2\frac{1}{4} \times 1\frac{3}{4}$ in.
Her Majesty The Queen
Painted for Charles I, from a portrait by Van Somer of 1618, probably to fill a gap in a frame of miniatures 'of your Ma^ts Progenitors'.

195. **Catherine Bruce, Countess of Dysart**
Watercolour on vellum: $8\frac{3}{4} \times 6\frac{1}{2}$ in. Signed and dated: *Hoskin.*/*1638.*
The Victoria and Albert Museum (Ham House)
The type is very close to Van Dyck's portrait of the Countess (at Petworth), but is probably an *ad vivum* portrait, its scale the result of the influence on Hoskins of the Van Dycks which he had been set to copy. It was highly prized by the Countess's descendants: in the 'Estimate' of pictures at Ham in 1679 it was valued at £40.

Daughter of Colonel Norman Bruce of Clackmannan and wife of William Murray, 1st Earl of Dysart.

196. **Henrietta Maria**
Watercolour on vellum: $3\frac{1}{2} \times 3$ in. Acquired for the royal collection in 1968.
Her Majesty The Queen
Painted for Charles I, probably in 1632, and recorded in his collection: 'Don by the life by Haskins . . . with a white feather and in a white laced dressing about her breast in a blewish purple habbitt and Carnation sleeves' (Van der Doort, p.106). On the back of the miniature is the monogram SC. It is difficult to dispute an attribution to Hoskins by Van der Doort, but the exceptionally high quality makes it tempting to consider at least the possibility that it was painted by Cooper when he was working with his uncle Hoskins.

197. **Charles I**
Watercolour on vellum, oval: $3 \times 2\frac{1}{2}$ in.
Signed: *I H fe.*
Her Majesty The Queen
Probably painted in the early years of the Civil War, possibly as late as 1647. In 1640 Hoskins had been granted an annuity of £200 by the King on condition that he worked for no other patron without his consent. By 1660 the Crown owed Hoskins over £4000. No.197 seems to have been a popular post-Van Dyckian image of the King.

198. **The Artist's Wife(?)**
Watercolour on vellum, oval: $2 \times 1\frac{5}{8}$ in. Signed with the monogram IH; repr. on p.116
Her Majesty The Queen
Probably painted *c.*1645. It has been plausibly suggested by Mrs. Daphne Foskett, on the basis of comparison with No.228, that the miniature is a portrait of the artist's wife, Sarah, who was Samuel Cooper's aunt and was still living in 1662.

199. **William Cavendish, 4th Earl and 1st Duke of Devonshire (1640–1707)**
Watercolour on vellum, oval: $3\frac{1}{4} \times 3$ in. Signed and dated: *IH*/*1644*; repr. on p.116
The Marquess of Exeter
Perhaps to be identified with one of the miniatures included in the goods given by the Countess of Devonshire (No.216) to her daughter, Lady Exeter, in 1690: 'A picture of the pre^sent Earle of Devonshire when a Child by Hoskins'. A fine example of Hoskins's style at this period, when his handling is

193

195

197   194   196

198

200
199

beginning to look a little less broad and atmospheric than the early work of Cooper.

200. Portrait of a Boy ('Master Cecil')
Watercolour on vellum, oval: 2⅜ × 2⅘ in.
The Marquess of Exeter
In the Countess of Devonshire's gift was 'A picture of a Boy playeing on Castinetts by Hoskins', which may be identical with No.200. It has, however, a breadth of modelling and delicacy of tone which would otherwise have justified a tentative attribution to Cooper.

201

201. The Three Children of Charles I
Watercolour on vellum: 3¼ × 4¹³⁄₁₆ in.
The Fitzwilliam Museum, Cambridge
Painted presumably in 1647, at the same period as No.172, when the children (James, Elizabeth and Henry) were in the custody of the Earl of Northumberland. Formerly attributed to Peter Oliver, who died in the last days of 1647, it is possible that No.172 should be attributed to Hoskins.

202. Henry Rich, Earl of Holland (1590–1649)
Watercolour on vellum, oval: 4⅝ × 3⅞ in.
The Victoria and Albert Museum (Ham House)
Almost certainly to be identified with the portrait of Holland 'of Old Hoskins' which appears in the 'Estimate' of pictures at Ham in 1679; but Mr Graham Reynolds considers that the boldness of style which it reveals would justify an attribution to Cooper in the 1630's (R.A., *The Age of Charles II*, 1960–1 (597)). A prominent courtier and favourite of the Queen who adopted a vacillating course in the Civil War which ended in his execution a few weeks after the King's.

SIR BALTHAZAR GERBIER (1591(?)–1667)

203. **George Villiers, 1st Duke of Buckingham**
Watercolour on vellum, oval: 5 × 3½ in. Signed and dated: *BGerbier/1618* (initials in monogram) and inscribed: *Fidei Coticula Crux.*
The Duke of Northumberland
Gerbier was an amateur painter in the service of the Duke and was actively employed in building up the collection, and supervising all artistic activity, at York House; as a dealer he was active when the royal collections were being dispersed. No.203 could have been drawn to celebrate Buckingham's appointment as Lord High Admiral on 28 January 1618/19.

LAURENCE HILLIARD (1582–1647/8)

204

204. **Portrait of an Elderly Man**
Watercolour on vellum, oval: 2¼ × 1⅝ in. Signed with the monogram LH; inscribed: *Ætatis suæ . . .* and dated *Ano Dni. 1640.*
The Fitzwilliam Museum, Cambridge
The fourth child of Nicholas Hilliard, Laurence was trained by his father as goldsmith and miniaturist and in 1608 was granted in reversion his father's office of Limner to the King. His right hand was badly damaged when he was beaten up by a gang of toughs in Holborn in 1622. No.204 is painted in the quiet, 'English', tradition which Laurence Hilliard inherited from his father: virtually unaffected by the influence of Peter Oliver or Hoskins and, unlike them, untouched by the influence of Van Dyck (E. Auerbach, *Nicholas Hilliard* (1961), pp. 224–32).

CORNELIUS JOHNSON (1593–1661)

205. **Portrait of a Man**
Oil on copper, oval: 3⅛ × 1 11/16 in. Inscribed on the back of the copper: *C. Johnson Fecit 1639.*
The Duke of Portland
Johnson, during his years in England, produced a number of miniature portraits in oil which are indistinguishable in feeling from his portraits on the scale of life and demonstrate the close links between painting on the two scales at this period (Goulding, No.78).

206

206. Thomas Hamilton, 2nd Earl of Haddington (1600–40)

Oil on copper, oval: height 1 $\frac{13}{16}$ in.

The Earl of Haddington   repr. on p.117

Painted *c*.1635. The sitter was an active Covenanter.

207. Portrait of a Man

Oil on copper: 9$\frac{3}{4}$ × 8 in. Stated to be signed and dated 1627.

The Marquess of Bath, Longleat

Hitherto identified as the Duke of Buckingham, No.207 is a good example of Johnson working on the miniature scale for sitters at half-length or more. A number of little full-lengths by him are also recorded.

EDWARD NORGATE (1581–1650)

208. Portrait of the Artist's Wife

Watercolour on vellum, oval: 2$\frac{5}{32}$ × 1$\frac{23}{32}$ in. Inscribed on the back by the artist: *Juditha Norgate . 1617 . æt: Non obijt sed abijt. Pudicitiæ, Pietatis, et Venustatis rarissimum decus . Suauissimæ Conjugi Ed: Norgate.*

The Victoria and Albert Museum

Norgate was an heraldic draughtsman and filled a number of posts at court. Keenly interested in the arts and in his own craft, he wrote the treatise *Miniatura*, inspired by Mayerne and dedicated to Arundel, which is second in importance only to Hilliard's *Arte of Limning*. He was involved in the negotiations with Jordaens in the 1630s and had provided Van Dyck with lodgings on his arrival in London. His wife's death is movingly recorded in the inscription he wrote on the back of her portrait. She was Judith Lanier, whom he had married in 1613 (C. Winter, *Elizabethan Miniatures* (1943), p.31).

JEAN PETITOT (1607–91)

209. George Villiers, 1st Duke of Buckingham

Enamel, oval: 2 × 1 $\frac{9}{16}$ in. Signed and dated on the back: *J. Petitot fe. 1640.*

The Duke of Portland

Petitot, a native of Geneva, is recorded in London between 1637 and 1643, officially as a servant of the Queen. Assisted by Mayerne, he developed and enriched the technique of enamel painting for portraits in miniature. He was probably actively encouraged by the King and may have had help from Van Dyck. Certainly his English works consist principally of copies from important court portraits. No.209 is taken from Honthorst's group of the Buckingham Family, painted in 1628 and hanging in the 1630's at Whitehall. Such a copy is seen hanging over the Duchess's heart in No.101. The enamel process would have made it an especially precious and unfading image (Goulding, No.279; R. Lightbown in the *Connoisseur*, vol.CLXVIII (1968), pp.82–91).

210. Charles I

Enamel, oval: 2 × 1 $\frac{9}{16}$ in. Signed and dated on the back: *J. Petitot fec. 1638.*

The Duke of Portland

Copied from a portrait by Van Dyck of which the original is not located; a good version is at Kingston Lacy (Goulding, No.275).

211. Henrietta Maria

Enamel, oval: 2 × 1 $\frac{9}{16}$ in. Signed and dated on the back: *J.P. f.1639.*

The Duke of Portland

Copied from a popular full-length pattern by Van Dyck of which the best-known, but not the original, version is in the royal collection; as a type it was probably first produced in 1636 (Goulding, No.276).

212. Rachel de Ruvigny, Countess of Southampton (1603–40)

Enamel: 9$\frac{3}{4}$ × 5$\frac{5}{8}$ in. Signed and dated: *Petitot fec^t. 1643.*

The Devonshire Collection, Chatsworth. Lent by the Trustees of the Chatsworth Settlement.

Copied from the portrait by Van Dyck of which the original is in the National Gallery of Victoria (*Catalogue* by U. Hoff (1967), pp.39–40). The design is one of those mentioned by Bellori ('in forma della Dea fortuna sedente sù'l globo della terra') and shows the Countess triumphant over death and fortune. 'La belle et vertueuse Huguenotte', daughter of the Seigneur de Ruvigny, she married in 1634, as her second husband, the 4th Earl of Southampton. Three of their five children died young, the eldest son in 1635.

SAMUEL COOPER (1609–72)

213. Margaret Lemon
    Watercolour on vellum, oval: $4\frac{3}{4} \times 3\frac{3}{4}$ in.
Signed: *SC*, and inscribed: *MARGARET* (in
monogram) *LEMON*; repr. on p.120
*The Fondation Custodia (Collection F. Lugt)
Institut Néerlandais, Paris.*
    Probably the earliest signed work by Cooper,
painted *c.*1635, at the time when the sitter was Van
Dyck's mistress: 'a dangerous woman', in the words
of Hollar, 'this demon of jealousy who caused the
most horrible scenes when ladies belonging to
London society had been sitting to her lover for their
portraits and who on one occasion in a fit of hysterics
had tried to bite Van Dyck's thumb off so as to pre-
vent him from ever painting again'. The miniature
shows astonishing maturity and an advance, in
atmosphere, design, and in the breadth and fluency
of his touch, on Cooper's predecessors and contemporaries, which indicate that Van Dyck had already
exercised a profound influence upon him.

214. John Leslie, 6th Earl of Rothes (1600–41)
    Watercolour on vellum, oval: height 2 in.
The Earl of Haddington
    Painted *c.*1635–40. The Earl was a strong
opponent of Episcopacy and prominent among the
early Covenanters.

215. Sir John Hamilton (b.1605)
    Watercolour on vellum, oval: height: $2\frac{1}{4}$ in.,
repr. on p.120
The Earl of Haddington
    Painted *c.*1635–40. Nos.214, 215, hitherto
attributed respectively to Hoskins and an unknown
artist, appear very close to the early work of Cooper,
in the subtlety of colour, the lucid design and the full
modelling of form that they display. The sitter was
the brother of the 2nd Earl of Haddington.

**216. Elizabeth Cecil, Countess of Devonshire
(c.1620–1689)**
    Watercolour on vellum: $6\frac{3}{8} \times 4\frac{7}{8}$ in. Signed and
dated: *Sa: Cooper/pinx . . A° 1642*; repr. p.121
The Marquess of Exeter
    An example, early in Cooper's career, of the
influence of Van Dyck both in scale and design as
well as in breadth of handling. The portrait can be
compared, in general terms, with Van Dyck's of the
same sitter, among the 'Countesses' at Petworth.
She was a daughter of the 2nd Earl of Salisbury and
married in 1639 the 3rd Earl of Devonshire; for her
son, see No.199.

209

214

215

217

217. **Portrait of a Man**

Watercolour on vellum, oval: $2\frac{7}{8} \times 2\frac{1}{4}$ in.
Signed and dated: *S: Cooper | fe: 1645* and
incised on the back: *Samuel Cooper | fecit
feberuaris | 1644 | ould stile*
Her Majesty The Queen

Formerly thought to be a portrait of Robert
Walker (see No.160). A superb example of the
sense of an actual physical presence, and of the
richness of tone and atmosphere, which set Cooper
on to a higher plane of excellence than any other
English miniaturist.

213

218. Anne St. John, Countess of Rochester (1614–96)

Watercolour on vellum, oval: $2\frac{5}{8} \times 2\frac{1}{8}$ in. Signed and dated: *S.C./1647*, and incribed on the back: *The Lady Rochester don by S Cooper in London.*

The Earl Spencer

Daughter of Sir John St. John; married *c*.1644, as her second husband, Henry Wilmot, 1st Earl of Rochester. She was the mother of the poet Rochester.

Nos. 217 and 218 indicate that, although he had absorbed so much from Van Dyck, Cooper's images are independent in that they never conform to a set of standard patterns. Each portrait is individually conceived to an extent rarely seen in the work of any other Stuart painter.

219. Henry Ireton (1611–51)

Watercolour on vellum, oval: $1\frac{31}{32} \times 1\frac{9}{16}$ in. Signed and dated: *S.C./1649*.

The Fitzwilliam Museum, Cambridge

The miniature was used by Walker when he put together his portrait of Ireton which is now in the National Portrait Gallery (3301). The sitter was one of the leading parliamentarian commanders and in 1646 married Cromwell's daughter Bridget. He died in Ireland as Lord Deputy.

218

216

219

220. Robert Dormer
Watercolour on vellum, oval: 2½ × 2 in. Signed and dated: *S.C./1650*.
Private Collection
Cooper was paid £12 for the miniature by the sitter on 8 September 1650. In its simple presentation it has affinities with Lely's portraits of the same period.

221. Oliver Cromwell
Watercolour on vellum, oval: 3⅛ × 2½ in.
The Duke of Buccleuch and Queensberry
Probably painted in the early 1650s. Cooper is known to have been working for Cromwell and his family in 1650. It is a study of the head, probably deliberately left unfinished like the five large post-Restoration studies in the royal collection. Such studies would be retained by the artist so that he could produce replicas of his prototype. There are a number of finished versions, copies and derivations of No.221 which was the most popular, and certainly the most illuminating, portrait of the sitter (D. Piper in *Walpole Society*, vol. XXXIV (1958), pp.31–32, 39).

DAVID DES GRANGES
(1611 or 13–1675(?))

222. Sir James Hamilton
Watercolour on vellum, oval: height 2 in. Signed: *DDG*.
The Earl of Haddington
The sitter was the second son of the 1st Earl of Haddington.

223. Christian Lindsay, Countess of Haddington (d.1704)
Watercolour on vellum, oval: height 2¼ in. Signed and dated: *DD.G/1648*.
The Earl of Haddington
Daughter of the Earl of Crawford and Lindsay, she married the 4th Earl of Haddington in 1648. Des Granges's earliest miniatures were copies after Van Dyck; his more individual works are competent, rather dry, essays in the manner of Hoskins.

224. Charles II
Watercolour on vellum, oval: height 2 in. Signed and dated: *DDG/1650*.
Private Collection
A copy in miniature of the portrait painted of

the young King in exile in The Hague by Hanneman in 1650. Des Granges was with the King as his official Limner, on the eve of his coronation in Scotland and produced for him a number of these small official images for distribution among his followers.

ARTIST UNKNOWN

225. **William Cavendish, 1st Duke of Newcastle (1593–1676)**
Watercolour on vellum, oval: 2 $\frac{13}{16}$ × 2 $\frac{1}{4}$ in.
The Duke of Portland
Probably painted in the early years of the Civil War, when the Earl (later the Marquess) was the King's principal commander in the north until his disastrous defeat at Marston Moor. One of the most accomplished and magnificent men of his time, a friend and patron of Van Dyck and a leading authority on the art of horsemanship, to which he devoted himself during his exile in Flanders (Goulding, No.156).

227

Samuel Cooper (1609–72)

226. **Thomas Alcock**

Black chalk on paper: $7 \times 4\frac{1}{2}$ in. Inscribed on the back-board of the frame by the sitter as drawn for him at the Earl of Westmorland's house at Apethorpe 'by the Greate, tho' little Limner, The then famous Mr Cooper of Covent Garden', when the sitter was eighteen.

The Visitors of the Ashmolean Museum, Oxford

Probably drawn *c*.1655 (Mrs Poole, *Catalogue of Portraits . . .*, vol. I (1912, pp.177–8).

227. **A Dead Child**

Black chalk, heightened with white, on paper: 7×5 in.; repr.on p.123
Private Collection

An early inscription on the back states that the child was one of Samuel Cooper's.

228. **Mrs. John Hoskins (?)**

Black chalk on paper: 11×9 in. Signed with the monogram SC.
Private Collection

The sitter is almost certainly the same as in Hoskins's miniature (No.198). Nos.226-8 are exhibited as examples of the growth of portrait-drawing in England under the Stuarts: drawings, that is to say, which were made in their own right and not in preparation for painted portraits.

Sculpture

NICHOLAS STONE (1587(?)–1647)

229. Orlando Gibbons (1583-1625)

Marble: height 20 in.

The Dean and Chapter of Canterbury Cathedral

The portrait-bust from the monument erected by Stone in the north aisle of the nave of the cathedral in 1626; the sitter's widow paid Stone £32 for it (W. L. Spiers in *Walpole Society*, vol. VII (1919), p.63). Stone was a prolific sculptor who produced a remarkable range of monumental sculpture, most of it imaginative in design and of distinguished quality. Composer and Organist of the Chapel Royal, he composed the music for the Queen's reception at Canterbury in 1625.

EDWARD MARSHALL (1598–1675)

230. Apollo

Alabastine: height 22 in.

Child & Co.

Originally placed above Ben Jonson's seat in the 'Apollo Room' of the Devil's Tavern and therefore made presumably before the poet's death in 1637; it was in the tavern that Jonson presided over his well-known literary gatherings. The bust reveals the obvious influence of the classical busts which had been acquired by Charles I, the Earl of Arundel and other collectors (Whinney, p.33).

HUBERT LE SUEUR (*fl.c.*1610–51)

231. Charles I

Bronze: height 27 in.

The Curators of the Bodleian Library, Oxford

Le Sueur, who had previously been in the service of the King of France, was in London by 1626. His portrait-busts of Charles I reflect the influence of the antiquities in the King's collection with which the sculptor was involved; they are also important in establishing the free-standing portrait-bust as a form of portrait in England. Of the bronzes of the King, which show the influence of Barthélemy Tremblay's bust of Henry IV, No.231 is the best documented. It was given to the University by William Laud in 1636 and apparently set up in its 'nest' in the Library in 1641 (Mrs Poole, *Catalogue*

232

of Portraits . . . , vol. I (1912), pp.44–45; Whinney, p.36).

232. Charles I
Bronze: height 27 in.; repr. on p.125
The National Trust (Stourhead)
Presumably made for the King *c*.1635. Placed in the Chair-Room at Whitehall: 'cast in brasse wth a helmett upon his head whereon a dragon' (Van der Doort, p.70).

233. James I
Bronze: height 68 in.
The Dean and Chapter of Winchester Cathedral

234. Charles I
Bronze: height 68 in.
The Dean and Chapter of Winchester Cathedral
The statues were made by contract (dated 17 June 1638) with the King to be placed in the niches in Inigo Jones's screen (now dismembered) in Winchester Cathedral. The sculptor was to receive £340 for his work and on 5 November 1639 was ordered to receive a further £40 for his charges in carrying them down to Winchester (Sainsbury, p.319). For Inigo's design for the screen, see Sir J. Summerson, *Inigo Jones* (1966), pp.125–6.

235. William Laud (1573-1645), Archbishop of Canterbury
Bronze: height 15 in. Inscribed with the sitter's name and age (62) and the date 1635.
The President and Fellows of St. John's College, Oxford
Successively Bishop of Bath and Wells, 1626, and London, 1628, and Archbishop of Canterbury, 1633, Laud was also the greatest of all Chancellors of Oxford University. He was a keen and scholarly collector and a munificent donor to the Bodleian Library; he presented his collection of 1242 MSS, including many volumes of Greek and Oriental MSS. He enlarged his own College of St. John's and beautified it with the Canterbury Quadrangle in which Le Sueur's bronze statues of the King and Queen are set in the niches above the entrances.

FRANCOIS DIEUSSART (*fl.*1622–61)

236. Charles I
Marble: height 34 in. Signed, dated and inscribed: *C.R. 1636./F. DIEUSSART. VALLON FECIT*   repr. on p.128
The Duke of Norfolk

237. Charles Louis, Elector Palatine (1617–80)
Marble: height 34¼ in. Inscribed with the sitter's titles, age (19) and the date (1637).
The Duke of Norfolk   repr. on p.128
The two busts were probably made for the Earl of Arundel. Charles Louis, the King's eldest surviving nephew, was in London with his brother Rupert in 1637 (they left early in July): 'a bad son, an unkind brother, and an unfaithful husband'.

The Fleming Dieussart had studied in Rome and his portrait busts are more animated in feeling and detail than those of Le Sueur, presumably because he had seen the work of Bernini. He designed for the Queen an elaborate machine for the display of the Holy Sacrament in her chapel at Somerset House (Whinney, p.38).

238. Henrietta Maria
Marble: height 21⅞ in. Dated: 1640.
The Royal Collection of Rosenborg Castle, Copenhagen
The attribution has been put forward by Mr Charles Avery. The bust is apparently based on Van Dyck's frontal portrait of the Queen, from the set of three designed to assist Bernini (see No.87). It would be interesting if a comparable commission, using the same painted sources, which had not been sent to Rome, had been given to, or assumed by, Dieussart.

GIAN LORENZO BERNINI (1598–1680)

239. Thomas Baker (1606–58)
Marble: height 32⅛ in.
The Victoria and Albert Museum
The sitter, whose sister married Sir Thomas Hanmer (No.103), was of Whittingham Hall, Fressingfield, Suffolk. Much interested in the arts, he travelled extensively in the 1630s and was in Rome in 1636. The accounts of Bernini making a bust of a young Englishman, who had been impressed (in Rome) with the marble of the King of England, are confused, as is the attribution of the bust. The material is admirably presented in Sir J. Pope-Hennessy and R. Lightbown, *Catalogue of Italian Sculpture in the Victoria and Albert Museum* (1964), vol. II, No. 638. The bust can probably be dated between 1637 and 1639; and the problem imposed by the papal ban on Bernini's carrying out private portraiture can be resolved by suggesting that he had already begun work on the bust and had completed

239

236

237

240

the head and gloves. The remainder was probably
finished by Andrea Bolgi.

In the Civil War Baker was active in his county on
the parliamentary side.

GEORG(?) LARSON

240. Venetia, Lady Digby

Bronze: height 22½ in. Signed: *G. Larson*. The
base is decorated with her arms and inscribed
with her name and: *VXOREM VIVAM
AMARE, VOLVPTAS EST:
DEFVNCTAM, RELIGIO*
Major J. M. Mills

Thought to be connected with the 'bust of
copper gilt' which Sir Kenelm erected on Lady
Digby's monument in Christ Church, Newgate
Street, and which was almost certainly destroyed.
For Lady Digby and Sir Kenelm's mourning tributes
to her, see Nos.187–9 (R.A., *British Portraits*,
1956–7 (169)).

Portrait Medals

SIMON PASSE (1595(?)–1647)

241. **Charles I when Prince of Wales.** Dated 1616; the type is close to the miniature of that date by Balthazar Gerbier in the Victoria and Albert Museum (*M.I.*, XVI, 4).

242. **George Villiers, 1st Duke of Buckingham.** Dated 1618, just after Buckingham's elevation to the Marquessate (*M.I.*, XVII, 5).

ARTIST UNKNOWN

243. **Anne of Denmark.** One of the medals complimentary to the Queen, issued presumably soon after her death. It provides one of the most vivid impresions of her appearance and character. On the reverse is inscribed her favourite device: *LA MIA GRANDEZZA DALL' ECCELSO* (*M.I.*, XVII, 7).

NICHOLAS BRIOT (1579/80–1646)

244. **Sir Theodore Turquet de Mayerne** (see No.42). Dated 1625, the year in which Briot arrived in London. In 1626 he received a warrant to make the Great Seal in accordance with a design which he had submitted to the King, whom he followed to York and Oxford during the Civil War (*M.I.*, XIX, 14).

245. **The Dominion of the Sea.** Dated 1630; issued to support the English claim to the dominion of the sea as laid out, for example, by John Selden in his *Mare Clausum*. A portrait of the King occupies the obverse of the medal (*M.I.*, XXI, 1).

CLAUDE WARIN (d.1654)

246. **Thomas Cary (1597–1634).** Dated 1633; signed.

247. **Margaret Cary.** Dated 1633; signed. Gentleman of the Bedchamber to Charles I and one of his most devoted followers. His widow married Sir Edward Herbert, Attorney-General to Charles I and Keeper of the Great Seal to the exiled Charles II. Warin's work for members of the court circle are without reverses and are among the earliest portrait-medals to be produced as such in England. Cary took charge of the medals which Charles I had inherited from his elder brother (*M.I.*, XXII, 9,10).

248. **William Blake (1603–67).** Dated 1634; signed.

249. **Anne Blake.** Dated 1634; signed. The sitter was a younger brother of Admiral Robert Blake; Chirographer of the Court of Common Pleas (*M.I.*, XXII, 11, 12).

250. **Richard Weston, 1st Earl of Portland (1577–1635).** Dated 1633; signed. Chancellor of the Exchequer and Lord Treasurer. The portrait reveals perhaps more clearly than those by Mytens and Van Dyck a personality which had 'lost the character of a bold, stout, and magnanimous man . . . and . . . fell under the reproach of being a man of big looks, and of a mean and abject spirit'. The medal was presumably designed to commemorate Portland's receiving the Garter in 1633 (*M.I.*, XXIII, 1).

251. **Endymion Porter (1587–1649).** Dated 1633; signed. A most significant figure in artistic circles. Porter had been in Buckingham's service; he accompanied him to Spain with Prince Charles in 1623; he was a patron of literature and the arts; and he was a close friend of Davenant, Herrick, Van Dyck, Rubens and Dobson. He was active on the King's behalf in acquiring pictures and negotiating with artists (*M.I.*, XXIII, 3; W. Vaughan, *Endymion Porter and William Dobson*, Tate Gallery (1970)).

JOHANN BLUM (*fl.c.*1630–60)

252. **The Marriage of William II, Prince of Orange, and Mary, Princess Royal.** The medal was struck in Holland to commemorate the marriage recorded by Van Dyck (No.110). The reverse shows the pair in a small Triumph of Peace over War (*M.I.*, XXIV, 12).

ARTIST UNKNOWN

253. **Thomas Wentworth, 1st Earl of Strafford (1593–1641).** Possibly by Thomas Rawlins, but in fact derived from one of the portraits by Van Dyck of the Earl, who was one of his most sensitive and lavish patrons; the best versions of the portrait are at Welbeck and Petworth (*M.I.*, XXIV, 14).

254. **Robert Devereux, 3rd Earl of Essex (1591–1646).** One of the Badges struck in 1642 to be given to his supporters by the Earl as general of the parliamentary forces (*M.I.*, XXV, 10).

255. **Prince Rupert.** A military badge of 1645, issued by the Prince to his followers. The portrait appears to be very close to that painted by Van Dyck in 1637, when the Prince was in London, and now in the Louvre (*M.I.*, XXVIII, 7).

THOMAS RAWLINS (*c.*1620–1670)

256. **'The Forlorn Hope'.** Issued by the Mint at Oxford in accordance with an order from the King that it should be worn on the breast of every man whose commanding officer cited as having done faithful service. It is decorated with portraits of the King and, on the reverse, his eldest son.

ARTIST UNKNOWN

257. **William Laud, Archbishop of Canterbury (1573–1645).** Almost certainly struck as a memorial of the Archbishop after his execution on 10 January 1645 (*M.I.*, XXVII, 9).

ABRAHAM SIMON (1617–92)

258. **Edward Hyde, 1st Earl of Clarendon (1609–74).** Struck in 1662 and therefore later than the period of this exhibition, the medal has been included as the finest portrait of the statesman and historian who produced the monumental and unrivalled single account of the Age of Charles I, the Civil War and the Restoration.

258

List of Lenders

Her Majesty The Queen 15, 63–73, 83, 84, 86, 87, 90, 93, 105, 109, 135–137, 178–181, 183–185, 190, 194, 196–198, 217

Her Majesty Queen Elizabeth The Queen Mother 175

Albertina, Vienna 11

Visitors of the **Ashmolean Museum**, Oxford 160, 163, 168, 226

Barber Institute of Fine Arts, University of Birmingham 120

The Marquess of **Bath**, Longleat 207

The Earl **Beauchamp** 191, 192

His Grace the Duke of **Bedford** and the Trustees of the Bedford Settled Estates 28, 29, 30, 141

Curators of the **Bodleian Library**, Oxford 25, 108, 231

Boymans-Van Beuningen Museum, Rotterdam 79

The Earl of **Bradford** 80, 81, 103, 138

Mrs Humphrey **Brand** 39

The Trustees of the **British Museum** 43, 58, 62, 113–115, 117–119, 123–133, 241–258

Edmund **Brudenell** 149

The Duke of **Buccleuch and Queensberry** 221

The Dean and Chapter of **Canterbury Cathedral** 229

John **Carleton** 6

A. D. R. **Caroe**, under Trust 177

Child & Co., London 230

The Governing Body of **Christ Church**, Oxford 10, 116

The Hon. Alan **Clark** 147

The Viscount **Cobham** 31, 166

Geoffrey **Coldham** 140

Courtauld Institute of Art, Lee Collection 170

Department of the Environment, Chiswick House 158

Devonshire Collection, Lent by the Trustees of the Chatsworth Settlement 45–57, 94, 111, 121, 193, 212